30 TICKETS TO PARADISE

A Young Man's Life-Changing Journey
To Every Ballpark In Baseball

A True Story

CODY KAUFMAN

Warning:

Some material in this book
is not suitable for children.

CONTENTS

"The one constant through all the years, Ray, has been baseball. America has rolled by like an army of steamrollers. It has been erased like a blackboard, rebuilt, and erased again. But baseball has marked the time. This field, this game, it's a part of our past, Ray. It reminds us of all that once was good, and it could be again. Oh... people will come Ray. People will most definitely come."

– Terence Mann (James Earl Jones)
in *Field of Dreams* (1989)

CHAPTER 1
The Crisis

It's a blazing hot afternoon in late-July 2011. For the umpteenth day in a row, I begin my twenty-one-mile commute from Burbank, California, to my apartment in Brentwood, a nice neighborhood in West Los Angeles. For the first eight miles, I battle constant stoplights and blinding sun as I make my way down Vanowen Street to I-405. Even though it's an obscure side route through the valley, it's my quickest option, taking me through the aesthetic sections of North Hollywood and Van Nuys. On the sidewalks, there are spray-painted plywood signs advertising ten-dollar oil changes, overweight vendors selling flowers and ice cream, and little Hispanic boys kicking soccer balls into chain-linked fences. One ball launches too high, drilling the windowless Econovan in front of me. This drag is nothing to look forward to after another meaningless day in the office. When I finally reach the I-405 onramp, I floor my gas pedal and head south.

As I merge onto the freeway from right-to-left, a red hatchback Honda Civic cuts me off, forcing me to slam on my brakes. The driver looks like the typical nineteen-year-old punk, blasting ghetto rap music on poorly installed subwoofers that he probably bought from a guy, who knew a guy, who stole them. A few minutes later, red taillights illuminate in front of me to the sight of vehicle smoke off the right-hand shoulder. From the fast lane, I notice a woman sitting on the guardrail while flames burst out of her charred SUV. She's on her phone, sobbing.

As I start ascending up Sepulveda Pass, I fall into highway hypnosis questioning my life. *My job? My girlfriend? Living in LA?* Two years ago, in the fall of 2009, I moved to Thailand to teach English after graduating from the University of California–Santa Barbara. A few weeks before I left, I met a girl, and we decided to do the long-distance thing for the six months that I was gone. She flew across the world to visit me during Christmas, and used that time to convince me to move to LA when I got back (something I would not have normally considered). When I finally returned to California in April 2010, I landed my job in Burbank, and moved five blocks away from her in Brentwood.

As I summit Sepulveda Pass and begin my descent into the LA basin, I mundanely ponder the negative feelings I've been forming in recent months. *Is this the life I want? Slaving through the same routine, the same office, and the same commute?* When I was abroad, I was off the map, learning about the world, and exploring the infinite possibilities that life could offer. But now, I'm more narrow-minded than ever before, with limited space and restricted opportunity. I'm like a tiger in a cage, mentally and physically incarcerated from the joy of running freely. While this comparison builds in my head, I exit the freeway onto Wilshire Boulevard West. I wait for a greasy-headed homeless man to push his shopping cart through the crosswalk. Then I turn right, looking forward to the end of another day.

A few blocks before my street, I pull up to the jammed

intersection of Wilshire and San Vicente. Waiting at the stoplight, I stare at cars on the opposite side of the median trying to go the other way. Eastbound Wilshire during rush hour is worse than the parking lot at Dodger Stadium, which allows me to closely study each miserable face that passes by. I roll down my window, lean into the smog, and imagine a day in the life of each zombie that crawls towards the freeway...

First up is an Asian gal driving a white Toyota Prius. She seriously looks like someone stole her puppy, and later found it dead in a ditch. I can't even look.

I then turn my attention to a white, curly-haired hipster with horn-rimmed glasses. He has blazed a crater in his headrest. His face is distraught, his skull cocked back in exhaustion. Either he hasn't slept in forty-two hours, or he's receiving the worst blowjob in the history of mankind.

My third subject is a well-presented African-American girl. If you asked a runway model to pose with the most expressionless face possible, this girl would nail it. There is no doubt she was the undisputed freeze tag champion on her elementary school playground.

Then comes the one that strikes me the deepest – a white male with strong features, maybe late-thirties or early-forties. The look on his face tells me he's just as miserable at home as he is in the office. At one time, he was probably a funny, inspiring, and spontaneous individual who thrived in athletics and social events. He graduated from college, and like everyone else, moved to LA, started a career, and got preoccupied with the choices that now define him. His twenties flew by, then his thirties, and now he's cemented into inevitable obligations – *career, marriage, mortgage, children, tuition, retirement*. It's the boardwalk of American society, but he dwells on the fact that he missed something along the way. It handcuffs his soul.

It's in this moment that I realize I'm staring at a carbon copy of my future, unless I make a change. My heart rate thumps as the stoplight turns green, and for the first time in a while, I feel motivated to take control of my destiny as I continue down Wilshire Boulevard.

I drive a few more blocks and make a right on Granville, where my apartment is two blocks north. I pull up behind a car that is parallel parking in a curbside spot. Nine-out-of-ten LA drivers would zip around this car, but I do the polite thing and wait. The streets are narrow and an oncoming car approaches. I wait for a couple seconds, before...

Beeeeeeeeeeeeeeeeeeeeeeeeeeeepppppppp!!!!!

The car behind me blares its horn in protest.

Beeeeeeeeeeeeeeeeeeeeeeeeeeeepppppppp!!!!!

Five seconds pass. I'm rattled.

Beeeeeeeeeeeeeeeeeeeeeeeeeeeepppppppp!!!!!

After eight seconds of continuous honking, I throw my throttle into park. Steam billows out of my ears.

Beeeeeeeeeeeeeeeeeeeeeeeeeeeepppppppp!!!!!

At the nine-second mark, I tear off my seatbelt, and on cue with the tenth second, I storm out of my car like I've been shot out of a canon. In a fit a rage, I charge at the black BMW behind me, stampeding directly towards the Persian face of the daddy's girl behind me. I'm at the boiling point of an absolute conniption.

"What the fuck is your problem?!" I scream over the hood of her car. "I'm waiting for that car to park!!!"

Although she has finally stopped honking, I kick and flail and scream at her like a horror movie character foreshadowing a murder. I flip her off eight inches from the driver's side window, veins bulging from my neck. When I eventually finish fuming at her bitchy expressions, I turn and walk away feeling lightheaded and dissatisfied. BMW Girl floors her accelerator to go around me, and I punt the backside of her 5-Series as she disappears up the street.

I get back in my car like a dog returning to its kennel, and drive the final block before diverting through a gate to my underground parking garage. I pull into my spot, turn off the ignition, and take a good hard look in the rear-view mirror. In the reflection, I see two eyes filled with fire. I see a character being tested. I see a person in the pivotal moment of a life-changing decision.

Los Angeles is dubbed the City of Angels, but I sometimes call it Satan's Playground – or better yet, Hell-A. The episode that had just transpired in the street made me realize something; I had become one of them, just another pissed off demon in the world. To any lucky spectator who just watched the drama unfold in the street, there was no difference between BMW Girl and I. We both complimented each other as road raging morons.

The stark reality is that BMW Girl and I would probably get along great if we met in a different circumstance. But like me, she's probably disgruntled with her life. She probably didn't see the car in front of me, and probably blew her fuse as quickly as I did. She's still a crazy lunatic, but no more than me for being a psychotic asshole seeking justice in the street. Satan's Playground has morphed me into a product of my crowded, stressful, and pretentious environment. My latest behavior is comparable to the crazy LA imbeciles I see on the six-o'clock news. I wasn't born like this, wasn't raised like this, and I certainly refuse to die like it. As former U.S. President Harry S. Truman famously coined: *The Buck Stops*

Here.

As I consider what has transpired, I put myself in the hot seat. I ask myself three critical questions aloud, right there in the parking garage, face-to-face with no one but myself.

Do you want to continue this career? "No."

Is your girlfriend the one? "No."

Do you want to spend the prime years of your life dwelling in Hell-A? "Absolutely not."

With that, I look back into the rear-view mirror with warrior-like conviction and declare the following two words: "Fuck. This." I shove my door open, and roar out of my car like a born-again tiger. I am escaping from this godforsaken cage.

CHAPTER 2
The Transition

The months following my quarter-life crisis turned out to be the most exciting period of my life. I quickly left my job, moved out of my apartment, and waved goodbye to my former life in Hell-A. My ex-girlfriend never looked as good as she did in my rear-view mirror.

Just days after leaving Los Angeles, I set my sights on an extraordinary physical challenge. I bought a road bicycle and embarked on a 625-mile trek up the California coast from my hometown of Temecula to San Francisco. At the end of each day, I stayed with family and friends who were kind enough to adopt me for a night. Networking to find hosts along the way turned out to be a valuable experience; at the time, I didn't realize how much it would benefit me later in life.

On my eighth day of riding, through what had to be divine intervention, I covered 135 miles along the edge of Big Sur from San Luis Obispo to Monterey. On the afternoon of my tenth day, I reached my personal finish line at the Golden Gate Bridge. Even though my butt felt like I had dropped the soap, the accomplishment offered a moment of clarity and a newly instilled sense of pride. It reassured me that I had made the best decision of my life, and served as a reminder of my ability to do great things.

After returning to Temecula and spending the holidays back home, I was ready for my next big adventure once the calendar struck 2012. Two of my best friends, Elliot and Mikey, had recently spent eleven months driving across South America in an eco-friendly, vegetable-oil van. Their pictures were breathtaking, their stories incredible, and it stirred an inner desire to check it out for myself. Without a set itinerary, I packed a bag and bought a one-way flight to Cartagena, Colombia.

When I arrived in early-February, I spent a week exploring the city before making my way to the annual "fiesta loca" known as Carnaval de Barranquilla (celebrated in the hometown of pop singer Shakira and former baseball player Edgar Rentería). I then continued northeast along the Caribbean coast to Santa Marta, where I had an arranged bartending gig waiting for me at a local hostel. When I arrived, though, the bar was fully staffed, so the owners sent me to their beach property an hour north. Suddenly, and completely unexpectedly, I found myself living on a beautiful, secluded Caribbean property next door to a surf camp.

The ensuing month at "the beach" was as awesome as it sounds. Aside from building a fence, helping with small landscaping projects, and making minor repairs, I had all the free time in the world to read, surf, talk, and play sports with the guests next door. I ate all of my meals at the surf camp, helped out in their kitchen, and honed my machete skills in the art of coconut cracking. There was no TV, no Internet, and the nearest road was a two-mile walk away. Despite being isolated from the outside world, I learned an incredible amount while I was there. I bonded closely with my surrounding friends and environment, and was in a complete state of peace by the time

I left.

Following these six weeks on the Atlantic coast of Colombia, I strapped up my backpack and continued my quest through South America. I went to Ecuador next, where I unexpectedly became friends with a young Japanese guy named Yuji. We came from faraway places, but the two of us shared a common age and an identical path ahead on the Gringo Trail. Despite our linguistic differences, Yuji and I decided it would be fun to travel together. We both had a knack for adventure, a thirst for beer, and a love for the outdoors.

Over the course of the next four weeks, Yuji and I mountain biked down a volcano, zip-lined through the jungle, rappelled down waterfalls, and trekked all over the northern Andes. I taught Yuji how to bargain, how to cook spaghetti, how to surf, and for the most part, how to speak English. These experiences reminded me of the important values in life, and ignited my overall spirit during long hours on the bus.

Yuji and I also shared a mutual passion for the sport of baseball. He would tell me stories about hardball in Japan while I told him tales of the Major Leagues. As our friendship developed, I became genuinely convinced that Yuji was my Japanese brother from another mother. Rather than my English lessons feeling like a chore, our conversations became an effortless task that was exclusive to baseball.

When the day eventually arrived for us to part ways, I gave Yuji a silent hug goodbye as tears rolled down his cheeks. Our departure helped me realize that I had discovered everything I was looking for in South America, stunning sights and great friendship. Even though I was building incredible memories on the Gringo Trail, I knew my time was quickly approaching to return to the United States. I missed my family, missed my friends, and after all of our conversations on the topic, I was really missing baseball.

One day not long after Yuji and I went our separate ways, I sat down to write an email to family and friends back home. As I typed it out, the words on the page blatantly reinforced how much I love traveling, how much I love baseball, and how much I love meeting new people. As I sat there staring my computer, a brilliant idea came to mind. In that moment, I knew exactly what I was destined to do during the summer ahead.

CHAPTER 3
The Decision (Not LeBron's)

In 1998, after San Diego clinched the National League Championship Series, the Padres released World Series tickets by phone. I was eleven-years-old then, but still remember my Dad waiting desperately on hold deep into the night. In the wee hours of the morning, he finally got through, and came up with two tickets to Game Four. Although the Padres lost four straight to the Yankees that year, attending the World Series with my Dad was a memory I'll never forget.

A few weeks after we went, my stepmom told me about a list my Dad keeps called *25 Things To Do Before I Die*. Nowadays, people call it a *Bucket List*, but I prefer his old-school title. A bucket list sounds like a scavenger hunt with the Easter Bunny, but my Dad's version begs for urgency. As my stepmom and I continued our conversation, she mentioned that my Dad had recently crossed off one of his most coveted priorities: *Take Cody to a Padres World Series game*. She emphasized to me that once the Padres had made it, nothing would stop him from reaching his goal. He seized the opportunity when it presented itself, and it was a little life lesson that I took to heart.

Years later, when I was nineteen and a sophomore in

college, I decided to sit down and make a list of my own. I got real creative with the title, naming it *25 Things To Do Before I Die*. I typed out twenty-five goals, saved the document inside a random folder, and completely forgot about it as years passed along.

As I stared at my e-mail on that fateful day in South America, I realized that my brilliant idea was actually one of my *25 Things To Do Before I Die*. It wasn't a "new idea" per se, but rather a timely reintroduction to a longtime dream – a personal "aha!" moment. As soon as the possibility struck me, I found the list on my computer and opened it for the first time in five years. To my astonishment, I had already achieved twenty-percent of my goals:

- Tour the California coast on bicycle.
- Live in another country.
- Climb Mt. Whitney.
- Run at least a half-marathon.
- Backpack South America.

As I scanned the remainder of the list, I quickly found the item I was looking for:

- **Attend a baseball game at all thirty Major League ballparks in one season.**

Just below that, another item complimented it perfectly:

- **Publish a book.**

Similar to my Dad's World Series goal, I knew I'd never

get a better window of opportunity. Mine was a grueling road trip, required significant time, and ironically, revolved around baseball. I knew that if I didn't do it then, I probably never would. With everything considered, I made an instantaneous decision to do the trip and write a book about it. Nothing was going to stop me from achieving my dream.

The pages you are about to read vicariously capture my experiences traveling across the United States and Canada during the summer of 2012. Although themed around baseball, my true stories highlight the people, places, history, and culture that I was introduced to along the way. Some chapters will make you laugh, some might make you cry, but all of them will bring you on the ultimate road trip of a lifetime. My adventures ahead chronicle the incredible events, insightful knowledge, and inspiring characters I met on my life-changing journey to visit every Major League ballpark in one season.

CHAPTER 4
Taking My Talents to South Beach (Not LeBron's)

On May 7, 2012, I fly out of South America and land in Miami to visit Kyle, one of my best friends from college. Three nights later, Cranberry and Mikey fly in from Boston and Chicago, respectively, for a four-man college reunion weekend. Before anything else, the four of us sit down to play *Rage Cage*, our favorite drinking game from undergrad. As quarters plink into shot glasses, I tell the guys stories from South America and reveal my summer plan to visit all thirty ballparks. Mikey, who is known to scorn the sport of baseball in favor of an up-tempo sport such as basketball, isn't listening as he labors through a miserable streak of beer chugging. He's losing badly.

"Mikey!" Kyle screams, "Raaaaaaage Caaaaaaage! Oh, and by the way, we're going to the Marlins game Sunday!"

The newly dubbed *Miami* Marlins recently opened their brand new, $515 million stadium. Marlins Park is at the old Orange Bowl site, two miles west of downtown in the Cuban community of Little Havana. The new venue is much more attractive and centrally located than the former residence at Sun Life Stadium[1], fifteen miles north in the suburb of Miami

Gardens.

On Sunday morning, after we all call home for Mother's Day, we ride the free Marlins shuttle from the UMiami Medical Campus to Marlins Park. Our first glimpse of the interior is a magnificent spectacle. It feels like the Houston Astrodome in 1965, which was considered at the time to be the Eighth Wonder of the World.

After taking our seats in Section 139, I spot two aquariums built into the backstop on each side of home plate. They hold more than a thousand gallons of saltwater and are protected by clear fiberglass. Behind the fence in left-center field is a seventy-foot tall, $2.5 million home run feature. Unofficially named the *Marlinator* by a poll in the Miami Herald, the sculpture moves, flashes, and sprays foamy water after each Marlins home run. With a mix of blue, aqua, orange, and pink, in addition to palm trees, a sun, and sea animals on the lower half, the *Marlinator* features giant marlins swinging back and forth over the top. It's like an inverted pendulum of SeaWorld exhibits, designed like something I would expect to find on Yoshi's Tropical Island in the video game *Mario Party 64*.

After the Seventh-Inning Stretch, Mikey and two of our other non-baseball-loving friends, Ivan and Hagen, decide to go home to watch the Heat playoff basketball game. While Kyle, Cranberry, and I take a stroll around the stadium, I tell them about my plan to eat a hot dog at each ballpark. When we approach the concession menu (which flips-flops between English and Spanish), I bypass the regular hot dog and instead select the $9.00 South Beach Hot Dog, better known as the SoBe Perro Caliente. This premium selection is smothered with Chipotle sauce, coleslaw and tomatoes to supplement the

---

[1] Sun Life Stadium is also home to the NFL's Miami Dolphins, as well as college football's annual Orange Bowl game.

16

condiment stand stocked with diced onions, relish, jalapenos, banana peppers, salsa, ketchup, and mustard. *Please take note: The "South Beach Hot Dog" is not to be confused with the "South Beach Diet."*

While I devour my first wiener of the summer, we watch the Mets score two runs in the top of the ninth inning to take a 4-2 lead over the Marlins. After the third out, I'm stunned as I witness a number of fans make a mass exodus for the parking lot. They should know better than to leave before their team comes to bat. After all, it was baseball legend Yogi Berra who coined the phrase, "It ain't over till it's over."

From underneath the *Marlinator* in left-center field, we cheer as Emilio Bonifacio leads off with a triple. Then John Buck walks. And Greg Dobbs singles. Suddenly it's 4-3 with no outs. With a runner on third base, Jose Reyes comes to bat and delivers a sacrifice fly. The runner tags up to tie the score 4-4!

Omar Infante pops up for the second out, but Hanley Ramirez follows with a walk. There are now runners on first and second base with two outs in the bottom of the ninth inning. The stadium is buzzing, the entertainment unpredictable. The hopeless fans that departed early stand clueless in the parking lot.

The Mets relief pitcher, their second of the inning, is clearly rattled. He hits Austin Kearns with the next pitch, sending him to first base. The bases are now loaded with two outs in the bottom of the ninth, every boy's sandlot fantasy.

Standing at six-foot-five, 248 pounds, Giancarlo Stanton steps into the batter's box with bright pink shoes and a bright pink bat. The ninth inning magic has electrified the crowd. I turn to tell Kyle and Cranberry that, "nothing would cap off my first stop better than..."

No sooner than the words leave my mouth, Giancarlo Stanton absolutely smashes the first pitch fastball. As a former center fielder, I forecast the trajectory as it sails through the air. From way behind the *Marlinator*, well beyond the outfield fence, my arms stretch over the concourse railing as the walk-off grand slam falls inches below my fingertips. The roar of the crowd is deafening, a no-doubter from the press box.

As the stadium explodes into euphoria, Kyle, Cranberry, and I celebrate the dramatic finish in the midst of the crowd. The *Marlinator* sprays water into the air, covering us with foam. With twenty-nine ballparks to go, this is the perfect ending to the very beginning. My summer of baseball has only just begun.

Celebrating the win underneath the Marlinator.

Game 1: Marlins Park, Miami, FL
May 13, 2012 – Mets 4, Marlins 8

Category	Rank	Comments
Best Design	14	In addition to a massive scoreboard, two aquariums, the *Marlinator*, and a retractable roof, Marlins Park is covered in world-renowned artwork.
Best View	16	Sliding glass panels over left field offer a direct view of downtown Miami.
Best Hot Dog	7	Tons of extras at the condiment stand. Skip the $9.00 SoBe Perro Caliente and load up the $6.00 regular hot dog instead.
Best Mascot	9	*Billy the Marlin* is an iconic prankster in Miami. Keep an eye out in the middle of the fifth inning.
Best Fans	30	Attendance has always been an issue in Miami. Tame crowd, and too many leave early.
Best-Looking Females	24	Miami's sexy, but the babes are in South Beach.
Best Entertainment	19	The sea animal costume race is a favorite for the youngsters.
Best Tradition	30	Fire sales – Management selling off all of its good players.
Best Feature	4	The $2.5 million *Marlinator* features jumping marlins, bright colors, and spouting geysers after each home run.
Final Rank	19th	Marlins Park is swanky like Miami nightlife, but the lack of tradition and devoted fanfare hurts the cause.

The Kaufman Ballpark Index (KBI)
How It Works

All thirty ballparks are ranked in my book at the end of their respective chapter. The ballparks are judged in nine individual categories: Best Design, Best View, Best Hot Dog, Best Mascot, Best Fans, Best-Looking Females, Best Entertainment, Best Tradition, and Best Feature.

In each category, I ranked the ballparks from 1–30 with "1" being the best and "30" being the worst. The "Final Rank" was determined by calculating an average score (with each category receiving equal weight), by which I added together all categories and divided the sum by nine. This cumulative ranking was then sorted (lowest average being the best) to determine the "Final Rank" of each ballpark in baseball.

Disclaimer: These assessments merely reflect my subjective analysis based upon personal experience. It is important to remember that each category (Best Mascot vs. Best View) is given equal weight; therefore, my final rankings may be contrary to popular opinion. The Kaufman Ballpark Index (KBI) is not designed to favor aesthetics only, but rather the overall game experience for a general fan.

Please don't call me or email me or fly across the country to bark at me because I "undervalued" your precious field. I will simply remind you that I dedicated three months of my life microscopically evaluating each category by recording observations, collecting information, and personally touring every ballpark. The KBI isn't the law of the land, but rather a theory being brought forward by yours truly. It's important to remember, though (ladies), that I'm always right. My advice: Enjoy the amusement!

CHAPTER 5
America's Finest City

In 1945, The Cubs' *Curse of the Billy Goat* was born when Billy Sianis, owner of Billy Goat Tavern in Chicago, brought his pet goat to a World Series game against the Tigers. Fans at Wrigley Field complained about the goat's odor, and security gave him a choice: Either the goat leaves, or you both leave. Sianis refused, and during his outrageous exit, he screamed, "Them Cubs, they aren't gonna win no more!" He later sent a telegram to Cubs owner Philip K. Wrigley, which read:

> *You are going to lose this World Series and you are never going to win another World Series again. You are never going to win a World Series again because you insulted my goat.*

Unlike the ongoing curse in Chicago, Boston's *Curse of the Bambino* was lifted when the Red Sox won the 2004 World Series. Previously winners of five World Series, the Red Sox were the most successful franchise in baseball until they sold Babe Ruth to the Yankees for $25,000 following the 1919 season. After acquiring the Bambino, the Yankees became the most iconic team in sports while the Red Sox suffered their eighty-six-year drought.

Although less publicized than the historic curses in Chicago and Boston, the sports curse in San Diego might be the saddest of all. San Diego is the largest city in the United States without a major sports championship (World Series, Super Bowl, NBA Finals, Stanley Cup), and it holds the longest drought of any city with two major sports franchises. The Rockets and Clippers of the NBA moved to Houston and Los Angeles in 1971 and 1984, respectively, and the pressure has mounted on the Padres and Chargers ever since.

The Chargers actually made it to Super Bowl XXIX, but lost 49-26 to the 49ers to conclude the 1994-'95 season. Eight members of that Super Bowl squad have since died, including San Diego's most beloved icon, Junior Seau. Fellow linebacker David Griggs struck a pole in 1995 after his vehicle veered off the highway. Running back Rodney Culver died with his wife in a 1996 Florida plane crash. They were returning home early from a vacation because they missed their kids. But the eeriest incident happened in 1998, when Doug Miller was struck by lightning, twice. A friend initially revived Miller through CPR, but moments later he was struck again. Tragically ironic is that Miller played his NFL career with two lightning bolts on his helmet.

Another hometown hero is Tony Gwynn. Gwynn's Padres made two appearances in the World Series, but lost to the Tigers in 1984 and to the Yankees in 1998. In 1994, Gwynn was on the verge of hitting a historic season batting average of .400, but the season was cut short late in the year when Major League Baseball abruptly went on strike. To make matters worse, the Padres are the only team besides the Marlins that haven't had a player hit for the cycle. They're also the only team in baseball that hasn't pitched a no-hitter or a perfect game.

As the evidence shows, San Diego hasn't had good fortune when it comes to sports. What it does have, however (in addition to great weather, people, and beaches), is *Harry The Heckler*, the most notorious fan in baseball. The Padres might not field the most talent, but they can rest assure they have the best fan. Harry has heckled left fielders for decades, and his appearance strikes an impression just as much as his jokes. Ron Burgundy (and Baxter too) would whimper if they ever saw Harry's handlebar mustache on the streets of San Diego.

There's not a left fielder in baseball who doesn't know about Harry The Heckler. Players expect him when they play in San Diego. Moises Alou always requested to play right field when his team came to town. When Lance Berkman played left field for the Astros, he gave Harry an autographed bat, which read: *To the best heckler in the league, well, the loudest anyway.*

Barry Bonds once gave Harry The Heckler a much harsher gift: a death threat. Bonds had pulled his inner groin on his way to first base, and began massaging it when he came out to left field later that inning. Harry yelled, "Barry, you're not hurt! You're just using that as an excuse to play with yourself in public!" The following night, Bonds approached the outfield wall to tell Harry that he'd beat him to death if he ever found him outside the park.

On the third of June, several weeks after returning home from Miami, my brother and I visit Petco Park to watch our beloved Padres play the Diamondbacks. After the game, I catch up with the man, the myth, the legend himself, Harry The Heckler:

What year did you start heckling at Padres games?
"My dad was in the Navy when he moved our family to San

Diego in 1961. That summer, he took my two older brothers and I to our first ballgame. Heckling comes naturally to me. I've always had a smart mouth and never have been one to hold opinions to myself. The same thing that makes me popular at games also used to get me in trouble when I was in school. When I discovered how much of an affect it had on the players, it just encouraged me to do more. My father taught me that cursing in front of people was wrong; he never did it himself. I often take my mother to ball games. I would never curse in front of her, so I'll never do it in front of someone else's mother, grandmother or kids. I also found that getting people to laugh affects the player a lot more than cursing. It really irritates me to hear fans cursing or saying something about a player's mom, wife, or kids. And I'm the first one to complain about them."

Left fielders know your reputation. Have you always sat out there, or do you move around?
"I used to sit in different seats years ago but found I had a lot more affect on players from the left field seats at the 'Murph'. I got season tickets in the front row, and when we moved downtown, it was a given that I'd stay there. I just like left field better than right field."

I love that you exclusively wear the brown, gold, and orange throwback colors. I'd be ecstatic if the new ownership group changed the uniforms back to this retro look (while keeping Camouflage Military Sundays). What are your thoughts?
"I love the camo look. As a disabled Vietnam Veteran, it makes me proud to have the Padres honor the military. I wish we could wear it on the road as an alternate jersey. I would like to go to a brown-and-yellow color with maybe some orange. I really

24

don't like that the current jerseys look so much like other teams."

Is your iconic mustache handlebar-style, or something else?

"It's a handlebar. I started wearing it decades ago because I thought it looked more western. I wear cowboy boots and dress with a western look."

I heard a rumor that you've developed a friendship with Chipper Jones over his career. Will you explain the story?

"For years, Chipper (or as I call him, Larry) played third base and could hear me in the outfield. In the early 2000's, he got up-close-and-personal when the Braves moved him to left field for two years. I told him I would lay off if he gave me a game-used bat, and when he came back the following year, a locker room attendant brought out a bat from the opposing dugout. He handed it to me and said, 'Chipper sent this to you'. When the game started, Larry came out to left field, and I asked him why he didn't personally bring out the bat. 'Are you embarrassed your fans will see it? How do I know it's your signature? You ought to bring out a ball so I can compare the siggys!' The next inning, Larry came out, walked to the warning track underneath me, and pulled a ball out of his pocket. He pointed at the signature and said, 'See, that's my autograph' as he tossed it to me. After we moved to Petco, Larry always made it a point to come over and talk to me when the Braves came to town."

Note: Following the 2012 season, Harry mentioned the following about Chipper Jones' retirement from baseball:

"During Larry's final series in San Diego, he elbowed his way through a throng of people in front of the Padres dugout before the game. He jumped over the fence, came up to the seats next to the dugout, and gave me a big hug goodbye."

What was the best bribe (or gift) that you've ever received from a player or team?

"I've been given many game-used bats (closing in on 200 now). Heath Bell gave me his jersey from the World Baseball Classic, which I treasure. In 2004, Brian Giles set me up with tickets to sit in the family section for the Padres' first ever series at Fenway Park and Yankee Stadium."

Do players talk back to you? What's the worst threat you've received?

"Many players have flipped me off and cursed at me, but Barry Bonds was the only one who threatened to beat me to death."

Do you believe in a San Diego Sports Curse?

"I don't know if it's a curse, but we just can't get a perfecto, a no-hitter, or a cycle. Maybe we just ticked off the baseball Gods."

Petco Park's Friar Frank is terrible. I'd like to see the Padres create the "California Hot Dog" (grilled dog, stuffed with French fries, melted cheddar, salsa fresca, guacamole and hot sauce in a toasted bun), modeled after San Diego's famous California Burrito. Will you be the first to publicly endorse my idea?

"I have a very limited diet, but the hot dogs at Petco shouldn't even be fed to dogs."

Your persona is legendary in San Diego, so I have to ask one last question. Are you related to, or do you know, the San Diego Chicken? If so, are you part of a secret society that also includes Ron Burgundy?

"I've seen the Chicken many times, but I've never met him. No one is supposed to know about the Burgundy Secret Society of Anchormen."

My brother (left) and I (right) at the Tony Gwynn statue outside Petco Park.

Game 2: Petco Park, San Diego, CA
June 3, 2012 – Diamondbacks 6, Padres 0

Category	Rank	Comments
Best Design	5	The restored Western Metal Supply Co. building stands over left field. The Park At The Park sprawls behind center field.
Best View	6	Near the bay facing beautiful downtown.
Best Hot Dog	28	You heard it from Harry. The Friar Frank is worse than dog food.
Best Mascot	8	The *Swinging Friar* has been the switch-hitting mascot since the late 1950's – friends with the San Diego Chicken.
Best Fans	20	Harry The Heckler provides a boost.
Best-Looking Females	2	Petco Park is full of kitties and bunnies. It's also in the Gaslamp District, the premiere nightlife destination in San Diego.
Best Entertainment	22	For the kids, "The Beach" is a giant sandbox behind the center field fence.
Best Tradition	14	Camouflage jerseys at every Sunday home game honor the military community in San Diego County.
Best Feature	7	The historic brick "Western Metal Supply Co." building serves as the left field foul pole and offers premium views.
Final Rank	9th	One-of-kind design, fantastic setting, and attractive city places Petco Park in the top ten.

CHAPTER 6
Orange County

On the fifth of June, two days after my visit to Petco Park, I drive to Anaheim with my friends AJ and Kevin. Although my hometown of Temecula is equidistant between Angel Stadium and Petco Park, I've never been drawn to the Angels, especially as they've morphed into the Yankees of the west.

In 2003, billionaire Arte Moreno bought the team from Disney for $180 million, becoming the first Hispanic to ever buy a major sports franchise. As owner, he has signed top-tier talent and secured a lucrative broadcasting contract with Fox Sports Net[2]. As a result, the team's payroll has exploded during his tenure. In 2012, the combined payroll of the Angels was approximately $155 million, nearly $100 million more than the San Diego Padres. In Oakland, Billy Beane's genius frugality has become famously termed as *Moneyball*. In contrast, I refer to the lavish spending in Orange County as *Arteball*.

The Angels do deserve credit for developing young talent through their farm system. Players such as Mike Trout,

---

[2] In the 2011–2012 offseason, the Angels secured a twenty-year television deal with Fox Sports worth three billion dollars.

Mark Trumbo, and Jered Weaver were all homegrown within the organization. Trumbo, who was born in Anaheim and played at nearby Villa Park High School, might be the most underrated slugger in the game. His Hercules-like power in batting practice makes him more fun to watch than the great Albert Pujols, who signed a ten-year, $240 million contract prior to the 2012 campaign. In comparison, Mark Trumbo[3] makes just $500,000 per season.

Despite Mr. Moreno's popularity with fans, he committed an act of baseball blasphemy in 2005 that caused major uproar in Orange County. In an effort to create a more global brand, Moreno changed the name of the team from the *Anaheim Angels* to the *Los Angeles Angels of Anaheim*, capitalizing on the team's proximity to the second largest metropolitan area in the United States. From a business perspective, changing the name expanded marketing reach to LA-based fans. It also made the team twice as heavenly, as the team name literally becomes *The Angels Angels* when "Los Angeles" is translated from Spanish to English.

For a reader unfamiliar with Southern California, it's difficult to truly comprehend the backlash that this caused. Imagine for a moment if the Oakland A's changed their name to the San Francisco A's. Or better yet, what if in 1956, Walter O'Malley decided to keep the Dodgers in Brooklyn, but become the *New York Dodgers?* In those days, the Giants were still in New York, where a heated rivalry was already brewing between the two clubs.

Both hypothetical scenarios would've started a war, which is exactly what the City of Anaheim did when they filed a lawsuit against Moreno in 2005. They eventually dropped the

---

[3] In 2012, Mark Trumbo led the Angels with 32 home runs.

case four years later, but it's interesting to note that "Los Angeles" does not appear anywhere inside of the stadium, or on any of the uniforms. Even during broadcasts, announcers simply refer to the team as the "Angels" or "Halos" in a concerted effort to maintain fidelity with the Orange County community.

Politically, socially, and everything in between, Orange County and LA are quite different despite being thirty miles apart. Not only did Moreno's decision contradict that, but it was also the second time in ten years that the team changed its geographic identify. From 1966–1996, they were the California Angels, but converted to the Anaheim Angels in 1997 when longtime owner Gene Autry sold the club to The Walt Disney Company. When this transaction occurred, the City of Anaheim agreed to contribute $30 million to help Disney remodel the stadium, under the condition that the word *Anaheim* be incorporated into the names of both the stadium and the team. This legally explains why the phonetically funky *Angel Stadium of **Anaheim*** is home to the *Los Angeles Angels of **Anaheim***.

When AJ, Kevin and I arrive to the ballpark, it's hard to imagine that the NFL's Los Angeles Rams played here from 1980–1994. After opening in 1966 for baseball, Anaheim Stadium was renovated from 1979–1980 to accommodate the Rams during their move from the LA Coliseum. When the Rams ditched town for St. Louis in 1995, it paved the way for Disney to revert it back to a baseball-only facility.

Interestingly enough, the Angels have actually played in two other stadiums since becoming Major League Baseball's first expansion team in 1961[4]. From 1962–1965, the Angels

---

[4] The Washington Senators (now the Texas Rangers) were also an expansion team in 1961.

paid rent to the Dodgers and played at Chavez Ravine, but in 1961, they played at the *original* Wrigley Field. Yes, you read that correctly. The original Wrigley Field.

Before joining Major League Baseball, the Angels were a team in the Pacific Coast League from 1903–1957. At the end of that period, Walter O'Malley, the same Walter O'Malley who moved the Dodgers from Brooklyn to Los Angeles prior to the 1958 season, owned the team. At one time, O'Malley had purchased the Angels from Philip K. Wrigley, the same Philip K. Wrigley who played an instrumental role in the *Curse of the Billy Goat* in Chicago. Philip K. Wrigley was the son of William Wrigley Jr., the chewing gum entrepreneur who became owner of the Cubs. In the early 1920's, the Cubs' top minor-league affiliate happened to be the Pacific Coast League Angels.

In 1925, William Wrigley Jr. decided to open a new ballpark for his Angels in South Central Los Angeles, on the block between San Pedro and Avalon Boulevard, in between 41st and 42nd Street. It had Spanish-style features and was designed as a smaller replica of his ballpark in Chicago, which at the time was simply known as *Cubs Park*. When construction finished for the Angels, the new Los Angeles ballpark was named *Wrigley Field*, more than a year before the Wrigley name was adopted at the friendly confines in Chicago.

When Major League Baseball granted Gene Autry's wish for an expansion team prior to the 1961 season, he purchased the naming rights of the Angels from Walter O'Malley, who had discontinued the Pacific Coast League team when he moved the Dodgers to Los Angeles. During their inaugural Major League season in 1961, the Angels resumed play at their old home at Wrigley Field in Los Angeles, before playing their next four seasons at Dodger Stadium. During these initial five years, Gene Autry's Major League expansion team was actually called the *Los Angeles Angels*. So, as it turns out, Arte Moreno was only restoring Southern California's baseball history. He didn't change the name; he simply reverted it back to its original.

My hometown friends Kevin (left) and AJ (right) with me (center) behind left field at Angel Stadium of Anaheim.

Game 3: Angel Stadium of Anaheim, Anaheim, CA
June 5, 2012 – Mariners 1, Angels 6

Category	Rank	Comments
Best Design	23	Two full-scale renovations make Angel Stadium seem a lot newer than 1966.
Best View	24	The 57 Freeway is an eyesore, but the distant mountains provide some sort of landscape.
Best Hot Dog	27	Angels Dog... Not so heavenly.
Best Mascot	27	The only place to find the rally monkey is at the exit through the gift shop.
Best Fans	22	Similar to the monkey, where'd all those thunder sticks go?
Best-Looking Females	3	In Orange County, the sweetest oranges come in pairs.
Best Entertainment	8	The Kiss Cam has caught on everywhere, but the Angels do it the best.
Best Tradition	18	Light up the halo! It illuminates on the "Big A" statue next to the freeway after every Angels victory.
Best Feature	15	The Disney-designed waterfall cascade in left-center field shoots off geysers and fireworks.
Final Rank	21st	No mascot, subpar hot dog, and random location tampered an otherwise decent score and fun venue.

CHAPTER 7
Hell-A

In the spring of 1966, my Dad was living in Oceanside, 100 miles south of Los Angeles. One day, while my Grandpa was serving in Vietnam, my Dad's two uncles took he and his cousin Mark to watch Sandy Koufax pitch at Dodger Stadium. Koufax had won four World Series with the Dodgers, including three since their arrival to LA in 1958. The season before, in 1965, Koufax had been a machine on the mound. He had pitched a perfect game on September 9th, and had won the Cy Young Award, the Triple Crown Award (most wins, most strikeouts, lowest ERA), and was the World Series MVP.

My Dad was nine years old when he watched Sandy Koufax pitch that night. He remembers sitting on the third base side, and he remembers his uncles drinking beer. It was a school night, and they had promised my Grandma that they would return little Larry home at a decent hour.

As the game ended, the four of them rushed outside to beat traffic. They walked and walked and walked, and looked and looked, but couldn't find the car. My great uncles bickered and debated over where they parked, eventually sitting down on a curb, convinced it was stolen. It wasn't until after every last car cleared out when they finally realized their Station Wagon was actually there the whole time, right smack in the middle of the parking lot. They left Chavez Ravine that night ninety minutes after the game, the last vehicle out of the gate.

I laughed when my Dad told me this story several months after I left LA. For whatever reason, it made me feel better about my boiling point meltdown with BMW Girl, and gave me reason to believe that my bloodline just doesn't fare well in LA. Or maybe we just love San Diego too much.

Regardless of beers consumed or a lineage jinx, the parking lot at Dodger Stadium is disorienting. Dodger Stadium is built into a hillside known as *Chavez Ravine*; therefore, the lot is terraced rather than flat. In Los Angeles, fans find their seating level in the parking lot before entering the ballpark. The gate behind home plate is in upper deck, while the outfield gates are at field level. It's like a lodge at a ski resort, except it's a massive baseball stadium that seats 56,000 people, built into the side of a hill.

The natural topography makes the design of Dodger Stadium one of the most unique places in baseball. It's the third oldest ballpark in the Major Leagues, behind the antiques of Fenway Park and Wrigley Field. It's also the only park in the National League with symmetrical dimensions, meaning the outfield fences are congruent on both sides of center field.

This is where I'm going to stop and start rolling the ball a different direction. I hate the Dodgers. When I found out I was on the Dodgers one year in Little League, I cried. And there's no crying in baseball. I wanted to quit the team and take a retro Padres brown-and-gold dump on my stupid uniform. I was forced to deal with it though, which is probably why I now own a shirt that reads: *DUCK THE FODGERS*. I suppose the sportsmanship values that I learned in Little

League didn't carry with me into adulthood.

With three ballparks already completed, I leave home on June thirteenth with my bag packed for the summer. I drive my car straight to Dodger Stadium for the Freeway Series, a gridlock matchup between the Dodgers and the Angels. I won't bore the details, but I'd like to end this chapter with two noteworthy observations from the game:

1) When *God Bless America* plays, please take off your hat. Fans are typically respectful of this rule during the pre-game National Anthem, but rarely do it during *God Bless America* in the seventh inning. It's my baseball pet peeve – drives me crazy.

2) Guys: Never, never, NEVER get on one knee and propose to your girlfriend on the jumbotron at a game. Ever. It shows you put in a lot of thought and still came up with a shitty idea. You're doomed for life. If you're so scared of her response that you have to coerce her in front of thousands of people, then you shouldn't be proposing. You know what I do when I see this happen? First, I puke up my hot dog, and then I scream for her to dump your ass in public. If *Cosmo* published an article called *Worst Places To Propose*, I guarantee sports venues would be at the top. I know it contradicts Nike's slogan, but seriously... Just don't do it.

I REFUSE TO INCLUDE A PICTURE OF DODGER STADIUM IN MY BOOK. ALSO, VIN SCULLY IS THE MOST BORING BROADCASTER IN BASEBALL.

Game 4: Dodger Stadium, Los Angeles, CA
June 13, 2012 – Angels 2, Dodgers 1

Category	Rank	Comments
Best Design	15	Earthquake friendly? Check. Built into a ravine? Check.
Best View	9	The rolling hills of Chavez Ravine provide a nice break from the smog and freeway traffic in Smell-A.
Best Hot Dog	25	The $5.00 Dodger Dog is long enough but not thick enough. Yeah, that's what she said.
Best Mascot	30	No mascot? Sad. Super sad.
Best Fans	18	True Dodger fans sit in the left field pavilion. The rest of you need to get off your iPhone.
Best-Looking Females	16	The hot chicks in LA are still at yoga by game time, and with traffic, it's already too late.
Best Entertainment	15	You know you're at Chavez Ravine when a Tupac, Dr. Dre, or Snoop Dogg song wins Dodger Jukebox on a nightly basis.
Best Tradition	15	*I Love LA* song? Vin Scully? Take your pick, but I wouldn't pick Vin Scully.
Best Feature	26	The "THINK BLUE" Hollywood-style sign built into the hill outside of the stadium.
Final Rank	22nd	Baseball's third oldest ballpark offers unique tradition without the old-school charm.

CHAPTER 8
East Bay

On Friday morning, two days after my visit to Dodger Stadium, I drive up I-5 to Northern California. On Saturday night, I attend a wedding in Redding, and on Sunday morning, I rush my wedding date back to the East Bay. She has to study for the bar exam, but more importantly, I need to get to Oakland for the A's game at one-o'clock. Since I hate going to games by myself, I ask my date's best friend to come with me. Susan is the biggest A's fan I know, and I figure she'll be a great tour guide at O.co Coliseum.

It's not until I arrive to Susan's house to pick her up when I realize I could not have been more wrong. To my utter surprise, she comes hobbling outside in a cumbersome walking boot. She's limping like a three-legged dog on its way to the park, happy to see the light of day, but crippled by disability. She probably feels like Clifford on his big day out. As I watch her teeter sideways on her favored leg, I realize I'm in for a challenging afternoon.

"Hi! How have you been?" she greets me.

"What did you do to yourself?" I interrupt, ignoring her question.

"Oh, I didn't tell you? I had foot surgery…"

"Are you sure you even want to come?" I ask, almost rudely.

"I'm fine! Let's do this."

Susan and I drive to the West Dublin BART station where we park my car and gingerly tortoise-walk to the platform. We hopscotch our way onto the train, and when we arrive to our stop, I drag Susan across the bridge towards the ballpark. On the way, I notice a beggar holding a cardboard sign:

Need money for karate lessons – Family kidnapped by ninjas!

As we arrive through the entrance gate, we're handed a Coco Crisp Chia Pet. It's a little figurine of the A's center fielder, and his Afro grows in the form of a plant. Talk about a ridiculous promo giveaway.

I then tell Susan about my mission to eat a hot dog from every ballpark. We're both hungry, so we find a concession stand along the first base side. I get in one line for my Coliseum Dog, and she gets in another for her popcorn chicken. Both lines are abnormally long, but today is Father's Day, so there are actually fans here for once. Finally, after fifteen long minutes of waiting, it's my turn at the register.

"Hi, I'd like one Coliseum Dog please."

"Sorry, we got no more," the lady informs me.

Seriously? You ran out of hot dogs? It's still the third inning!

Susan already has her popcorn chicken in hand, and agrees to hobble over to the concession stands near our seats in the outfield. I figure it'll be less crowded with shorter lines.

When Susan and I get over there, though, we realize that the A's don't have a single concession stand along their outfield concourse. Not a single one. Being that I'm now

40

empty-handed out in Timbuktu[5], it forces Susan and I to continue all the way around to the third base side. I'm starting to feel really sorry for her; not only has she gimped three-quarters of the way around the ballpark for nothing, but her dog food is getting cold. Aside from that, I don't have my actual hot dog. Eventually, we reach another concession stand along the left field line. The line here is just as long, but we endure the ten-minute wait. Finally, I reach the front.

"Hi there, one Coliseum Dog please."

"Sorry sir, but we're actually out of those," the man replies.

"You're out too?"

"We have no more buns. There's another stand you can check a little further down."

I'm flabbergasted at this point, and realize I'm leading my handicapped tour guide on a tour of my own. Susan tries to lighten my visible frustration, which is a clear physiological result of my impatient appetite. We go a little bit further down and find the only concession stand that we've yet to visit. Without hesitation, I cut the line and interrupt some grandpa trying to order.

"Do you have Coliseum Dogs?" I bluntly ask the cashier.

"Nah man, the whole stadium is outta buns."

More rattled than the San Andreas Fault, I oppress my shaken frustration and turn to Susan. She has this look on her face like she's waiting for a bomb to explode. Then she delicately asks me a question.

"So, what are you gonna do now?"

---

[5] Timbuktu is an actual city on the southern edge of the Sahara Desert in the African nation of Mali. Living up to its reputation as a figure of speech in the English language, Timbuktu is in the middle of nowhere.

"Well first," I respond, "I'm gonna rank the Coliseum Dog as the worst thing in baseball."

"And then what?" she giggles.

"Probably steal some of your popcorn chicken."

With the Padres in town against the A's, Susan and I were a discordant duo in the already rowdy left field bleachers. If only her walking boot were visible in this photo...

Game 5: O.co Coliseum, Oakland, CA
June 17, 2012 – Padres 2, A's 1

Category	Rank	Comments
Best Design	29	It's the fourth oldest venue in baseball, with a huge foul territory, and a relatively small scoreboard.
Best View	29	O.co Coliseum is completely enclosed. There's nothing to look out upon.
Best Hot Dog	30	I have my doubts that the Coliseum Dog even exists.
Best Mascot	16	*Stomper* is the A's peanut-loving elephant. Follow him on Twitter @Stomper00.
Best Fans	11	The bleachers are loud and passionate with costumes, comedy, and giant flags.
Best-Looking Females	23	It's Oakland, but it's also the East Bay. You're bound to find some diamonds in the rough.
Best Entertainment	29	The old school dot races of red, white, and blue seem to get the fans pumped.
Best Tradition	29	A fan named Krazy George supposedly invented "The Wave" and sometimes brings his banjo. He's a staple.
Best Feature	30	O.co doubles as a football stadium, overlapping with the Raiders in the late summer and early fall.
Final Rank	30th	O.co Coliseum is dumpy and weathered, with old school charm. It's the last of the cookie cutter football/baseball hybrid stadiums, keeping the 80's vibe alive.

CHAPTER 9
Gold Rush

It's pitch dark in the lower Sierra Nevada Mountains, 150 miles northeast of AT&T Park. Seventy-two hours ago, I was watching the Giants close out a win against Dodgers, but now, I'm crouched behind a thick row of bushes in the middle of the woods. As I wait in position on this warm summer night, my heart thumps anxiously.

Ten meters to my right, Kyle is settled amid bushy shrubs. Susan is close to him, silent as the night, crouched behind a wall at the top of a long driveway. On the other side of the road, Cranberry waits motionless in a ditch. His sidekick Carlos hides behind a boulder. They're like Batman and Robin in the shadows of the night.

Minutes pass without movement. Then, like a distant lighthouse from a ship, we see a faint light through the woods. As it approaches, I identify the target as my team awaits the signal. It comes towards us from the road to my left. *Thirty meters, twenty meters.* The vehicle slows down, presumably looking for a driveway. *Ten meters...*

"FIRE!!!" I yell.

As the vehicle stops in front of us, I cock and fire through the darkness. I hear the sound of five direct hits echoing off aluminum, the same way a fastball slaps into a catcher's mitt. *Ker-ploosh, ker-ploosh! Kerploosh! Kerploosh! Kerploosh!*

Suddenly, the tires squeal on the asphalt as the vehicle roars out of sight. With it now over, we gather at the top of the driveway, victorious. We then proceed back down the driveway and go inside the house.

Moments later and a mile up the road, Griswold and Eddie sit in their car, freaked out. They thought they knew which house it was, but maybe they were wrong. Feeling a little lost, Griswold gives me a call. I answer the phone inside the living room.

Me: "Hey buddayyyy, you guys gettin' close?

Griswold: "Hey, did you guys just hit us with water balloons?"

Me: "You just got water ballooned? Seriously??"

Griswold: "Yeah. It wasn't you guys?!"

I turn to my army and spill the news with bewilderment, "Griswold and Eddie just got water ballooned!"

Kyle responds emphatically, "No way, are you serious? Where they at?" I turn my attention back to the phone.

Me: "Nah, man. We're just drinkin' in the house. What happened?"

Griswold: "Really? I thought we were at the right place, but maybe not."

Me: "Hmm… we did actually hear some kids running around earlier, but it's been a while."

Griswold: "Alright, well, we went up the road. We got a little confused."

Griswold and Eddie start the car and drive back down the hill, excited for the most fun-filled, old-fashioned college reunion weekend ever at Kyle's lake house. They're familiar with the neighborhood, but are challenged by tonight's darkness. This time, they turn off their headlights and drive cautiously down the street.

They quietly pull up to the top of a long driveway, and spy us mingling down on the front porch. At the top of the hill, they clandestinely park their car and grab two beers from their backseat cooler. Then, ever so discreetly, they tiptoe down the driveway without making a sound. They can't see our faces yet, but they've planned a special surprise.

As soon as they reach into view, they strip off their shirts and drop their pants. On the edge of the light, they obnoxiously crack open their beers. In the same tone as Sloth from the movie *The Goonies*, Eddie bellows, "Hey youuu guuuyyyyssssss!!"

Everyone on the porch looks up. Halfway down the driveway, there are two grown-ass men, completely naked, shaking and spraying beer onto each other like they just won the loony farm World Series. Griswold displays his "mangina" while Eddie swings his penis like a jump rope and throws his beer through the air. They scream and flail their arms like little girls.

At some point during the dance-off, Griswold and Eddie focus on the shocked faces of their audience and realize something has gone terribly awry. They don't recognize anyone. None of us are laughing. That's because we're actually sitting in the living room... two houses down the street!

In panicked shock, they turn and sprint up the hill, desperately trying to tug up their trousers. Both of them trip over their own feet and crash to the ground, mooning their onlookers. They manage to push themselves up and penguin waddle the rest of the way, but do so in terror. For the second time in fifteen minutes, they're freaked out, and peel out the tires into the night.

Back in the house, ten minutes have passed since I last spoke with Griswold. I call him.

Griswold (panting): "I need you to come get us."

Me: "Are you guys finally here?"

Griswold: "You wouldn't believe what just happened. I'll tell you when we get there."

As they loop back around for the third time, I flag them into the actual driveway. Griswold and Eddie frantically explain their story as tears roll down my face in hysterical laughter. In a moment of pride, Griswold says, "Even after we talked, I was convinced it was you, so we thought for sure we were at the right house when we saw those people outside." Then he pauses. "But whoever those kids are, at least we got 'em back!"

As we proceed into the house, Griswold spots a cooler next to the front door. We all watch discreetly, hoping he'll fall for the bait. We maintain our composure as he leans down to open the lid…

Resting inside is a Smirnoff Ice[6], and a dozen dark green water balloons.

---

[6] "Icing" is a drink chugging phenomenon that went viral across college campuses in 2010.

Phil, Kyle, Me, and Kurt (left to right) following the Giants win over the Dodgers.

Yeah, that's right.

Game 6: AT&T Park, San Francisco, CA
June 26, 2012 – Dodgers 1, Giants 2

Category	Rank	Comments
Best Design	2	The outfield concourse is a bayside boardwalk. And that's just the beginning.
Best View	1	The splash home run is a reminder that the Giants have the most pristine waterfront real estate in baseball.
Best Hot Dog	14	$5.00 Giants Dog is slightly above average.
Best Mascot	7	*Lou Seal* gets bonus points for being an iconic sea animal in San Francisco.
Best Fans	2	This was the 121st consecutive sellout at AT&T Park. That speaks volumes, literally.
Best-Looking Females	19	The San Francisco culture is a global melting pot. So is the female outlook. It's hit and miss.
Best Entertainment	23	Considering the rest of the experience, the scoreboard entertainment is a mild afterthought.
Best Tradition	8	"Lights" by *Journey* in the middle of the eighth inning, followed by *Frank Sinatra* after every game.
Best Feature	16	Fans can slide down the giant Coca-Cola bottle along the left field boardwalk.
Final Rank	1st	AT&T Park gets a lot of hype, and credit is due where credit is deserved. Incredible park, incredible location.

CHAPTER 10
Pacific Northwest

During the early 1840's in New York City, Alexander Cartwright invented[7] the game "base ball" while working as a volunteer firefighter at Knickerbocker Engine Company 12. An adaptation of "town ball", the Knickerbockers initially played the new game in an empty lot near Fourth Avenue and 27th Street in Manhattan. When the lot closed in 1845, Cartwright began searching elsewhere.

In 1846, Cartwright established the Knickerbocker Base Ball Club after he found a new park across the Hudson River. Some players wanted to stay closer to home, and the conflict of interest led to the formation of the New York Nine.

On June 19, 1846, the New York Nine beat the New York Knickerbockers 23-1 in the first organized baseball game ever recorded. Alexander Cartwright umpired the contest, and reportedly fined a player six cents for cursing. The historic game took place in Hoboken, New Jersey, at a park famously known as *Elysian Fields*.

In Greek Mythology, the term *Elysian Fields* represents

---

[7] On June 3, 1953, U.S Congress officially declared Alexander Cartwright as the inventor of the modern game of baseball.

the blessed and beautiful land where demigods, heroes, and righteous souls retreat in the afterlife. In baseball, it represents the birthplace of our national pastime, a sport ironically known to immortalize its legends by "enshrining" them into the Hall of Fame. In the sport of golf, the fairway of the 14th hole at the Old Course at St. Andrews in Scotland is nicknamed Elysian Fields, which is also the name of a New Orleans neighborhood in the novel *A Streetcar Named Desire*. There's even a famous street in Europe named after Elysian Fields. It's in Paris, better known as *Avenue des Champs-Élysées*.

I've never been to any of the aforementioned places, but right now I'm sitting at Elysian Fields in Seattle, a popular bar down the street from Safeco Field. Late last night, I drove from Kyle's lake house to San Jose, where his family has been kind enough to keep my car for the summer. At sunrise, Kyle drove me to the San Jose Airport, where my flight attendant excitedly announced shortly before takeoff that we were inside the "original Shamu-painted aircraft of Southwest Airlines!" *Let. Me. Sleep.*

The arrival flight my brother took from San Diego this morning landed five minutes after mine, and his friend Todd picked us up at the SeaTac Airport. Todd and his wife live across the Puget Sound on Bainbridge Island, and we've come to Seattle to celebrate the Fourth of July with a week of salmon fishing, crab-trapping, boating, barbequing, and of course, Mariners baseball. We've spent the better part of today doing typical Seattle tourist things: Pike Place, the Space Needle, food trucks, and the Redhook Brewery, which trades under the ticker symbol "BREW" on NASDAQ.

At six-o'clock, we close our tab at Elysian Fields and walk down the street to Pyramid Brewing Company, which is directly across the street from Safeco Field. Prior to every game, Pyramid hosts a tailgate festivity with an outdoor beer garden, Cornhole boards (sometimes called "bags"), and live music. After forty more minutes here, we finally cross the street, pass through the gates at Safeco Field, and find our seats near the third base line.

Unbeknownst to me, I quickly discover that Seattle is home to a group of rowdy and passionate supporters notoriously known as *The King's Court*. The massive mob shows up each time Felix Hernandez is scheduled to pitch, and completely conquers three designated sections near the left field foul pole. Every person in The King's Court wears matching royal blue T-shirts and flashes identical "K" signs[8] after each one of "King" Felix's strikeouts. Their intensity rivals the Duke basketball student section, which is mindboggling considering the Mariners are an underperforming team in early-July. Every time "King" Felix gets two strikes on a batter, the King's Court chants "K! - K! - K! - K!" leading up to the next pitch, which booms throughout the stadium. When the batter strikes out, they erupt like a bunch of peasants who just witnessed a lynching – absolute mayhem. They're likely the same breed of crazy soccer fans that the Seattle Sounders attract. Tonight, adding fuel to their own fire, Felix Hernandez records seven strikeouts through his first three innings. The King's Court is partying like they just beheaded Ned Stark in *Game of Thrones*.

By the end of the sixth inning, however, it's Baltimore's Wei-Yen Chen who is making all the noise. It's being whispered throughout the crowd that Chen is only nine outs

---

[8] In baseball scorekeeping, the symbol "K" signifies a swinging strikeout. A backwards "K" is recorded when a batter strikes out looking. In the King's Court, the "K" is also symbolic for "King" Felix Hernandez, who recorded 671 strikeouts between the 2009–2011 seasons.

away from a perfect game. In the bottom of the seventh, he records one out before getting ahead, one ball and two strikes, against the second batter of the inning. On the next pitch, he throws ball two, and follows it with ball three. Under normal circumstances with a full count, a pitcher might resort to a high heater or a nasty slider. But in this particular situation, with a perfect game in jeopardy, dancing around the strike zone is not an option.

Unfortunately for Wei-Yen Chen, all 16,270 fans at Safeco Field know exactly which pitch is coming next. Seattle's Casper Wells knows it, too. Chen throws the ensuing fastball, right down the pipe, and it's catapulted into the upper deck beyond the left field fence. The home run spoils both the perfect game and the shutout, and actually fuels a late-rally by the Mariners. Ultimately, the Orioles retake the lead in the top of the ninth, and hold on for the 5-4 win.

Earlier in the evening, just before we entered the ballpark, I did something that I had no idea would impact the rest of my journey. My brother, Todd, and I had four tickets, so I walked over to the Mariners ticket counter with the extra. I scanned people waiting in line and identified a young, homely-looking kid wearing a black leather jacket. I wasted no time, and approached him immediately.

"Excuse me, are you by yourself?" I asked, tapping him on the shoulder.

He spun around unexpectedly.

"I have an extra ticket," I continued, "If you want it."

His response was dire. "Twelve bucks! I've got twelve bucks right here. That's all I have." He held out all of the cash in his hand with glowing desperation.

This brought a huge smile to my face, because I was

already set on my selling price.

"Actually, it's free," I responded. "I just wanted to give it to you."

At that very moment, the baseball gods, or possibly the Greek gods, must have been watching over us from Elysian Fields. Little did I know then, but my ticket karma for the rest of the trip would be staggering. The young, homely-looking fella in the black leather jacket tucked the cash back in his pocket, and gave me the most joyous hug I had received all year.

Todd, my brother, and I (left to right), enjoying the summer evening at Safeco Field.

Game 7: Safeco Field, Seattle, WA
July 3, 2012 – Orioles 5, Mariners 4

Category	Rank	Comments
Best Design	16	Safeco has a massive retractable roof and a popular beer garden behind center field.
Best View	15	Sit on the south side of the ballpark for a view of CenturyLink Field and downtown.
Best Hot Dog	17	Mariners Dog has a large wiener, tasty toppings, and an awful bun. FYI – you can pay the $6.25 in Canadian currency.
Best Mascot	1	Trivia: Who's broken more bones crashing into the center field fence? Ken Griffey Jr. or *Mariner Moose*?
Best Fans	17	If the M's trade King Felix, they also lose their devoted *King's Court*, and that'd be a shame.
Best-Looking Females	4	Some of the hottest girls yet. Also some of the worst. The hot ones were really hot though.
Best Entertainment	4	Great entertainment between innings. Who knew Ichiro Suzuki's favorite actor is Hugh Grant?
Best Tradition	28	Losing? I'm kidding. Maybe the Moose Call?
Best Feature	28	"The Mitt" is an iconic 9-foot-tall bronze statue outside the northwest gate.
Final Rank	16th	Safeco is actually a great baseball venue. I bet the playoff atmosphere would be epic if that ever happens again someday.

CHAPTER 11
Mile High City

Writing is related to marketing in the sense that it's important to understand your target market. Since this book is themed around baseball, I can philosophically assume that my readers like baseball. With that, I can apply deductive reasoning using my own values to come up with the following proof: *If* my readers like baseball, *then* they also like beer.

My high school geometry teacher, Mr. McBride, would probably point out that this "if-then" statement is false. I failed to directly prove that anyone who likes baseball also likes beer. Therefore, I can't objectively conclude that all of my readers drink beer. I understand the objection, but to any philosopher, I would rebuttal with this: *If* you think my proof is false, *then* you've never been to Denver.

To my readers who aren't big baseball fans, there's a good chance you at least like beer. At the bare minimum, I know the following conditional proof is true: *If* you are a man, *then* you have a penis, and *if* you have a penis, *then* you drink beer. That fact alone takes care of fifty percent of the world's population. *If* you disagree with me, *then* you're either, a) lying to yourself, b) a saint, or c) allergic to gluten. After all, it was indeed Benjamin Franklin who once said, "Beer is living *proof* that God loves us and wants us to be happy." And one thing is for damn sure: You can't argue with the reasoning of Benjamin Franklin.

Beer connoisseurs usually enjoy beer history, which is why I'd like to open the Denver chapter with a little bit of trivia. Some of you may already know this, but I want the rest of you to put on your beer goggles and ask yourselves the following question: Where in the United States was Blue Moon created?

The Blue Moon Brewing Company is a division of MillerCoors LLC, which is a joint venture between SABMiller and Molson Coors. MillerCoors is headquartered out of Chicago, and was formed in 2008 to increase competition with Anhueser-Busch InBev in North America. SABMiller, operated out of London, formed when SAB ("South African Breweries") purchased the Miller Brewing Company in 2002. Miller Brewing Company, however, continues to operate independently in Milwaukee, Wisconsin. In 2005, Molson Canada merged with the Coors Brewing Company, but they continue to operate independently out of Montreal and Denver, respectively. Nevertheless, with all these possibilities, the question still begs: Where did Blue Moon come from?

If you guessed underneath Coors Field, *then* you are correct. Blue Moon, a Belgian-style wheat beer, was actually invented by Keith Villa at the Sandlot Brewery at Coors Field. Today, the microbrewery and restaurant has become the Blue Moon Brewery at The Sandlot, and is accessible behind the right field stands at Rockies games, or from Blake Street on the west side of the ballpark. It's a random bit of trivia, but it's good beer knowledge next time you're at the bar.

The holy grail of microbreweries, though, is in Portland, Oregon, which is where I am after my visit to Seattle.

I've been here for a few days visiting my uncle and my Grandpa, resting and preparing to launch into my sixty-day trip that will cover the remaining twenty-three ballparks. Up until this point, I've excluded two critical details that will shape the outlook of my trip: Finances and transportation.

While I was backpacking through South America earlier in the spring, I mentioned my ballpark idea to two American girls in my hostel who had just finished a twenty-seven month deployment in the Peace Corps. I told them that I was considering a motorcycle for gas price efficiency, and they both looked at me like I was nuts. Which I was. Alternatively, one of them offered a better, cheaper, and more feasible solution – Buying a fixed-term bus pass.

Rationality told me that this trip was not in my best career or financial interest, but the devil's advocate in me screamed, "You're twenty-five with no obligations! Just do it!" When I visited Greyhound's website to research various options, my dream became solidified. Well within my budget was the sixty-day Greyhound Discovery Pass, which granted me unlimited bus trips throughout North America for a grand total of $564.

Although I have paid in advance, I don't pick up my Discovery Pass until I arrive to the Portland Greyhound station on the twelfth of July. I'm there an hour early, which gives me ample time to scout the suspicious breed of creatures I'll be traveling with for the next two months. I'm excited but apprehensive, particularly when I realize that I'm about to ride thirty hours to Denver, with some *freaks*.

For the rest of that Thursday and all day Friday, I endure a range of emotions that can only be described as miserable, hilarious, antagonizing, and ridiculous. That first bus trip would be the longest but funniest of the summer. Here are some actual quotes highlighting my thirty-hour circus trailer ride to the Mile High City:

From my awkward neighbor sitting next to me while stopped in The Dalles, Oregon:
"So, where ya headed?"
"Denver."
"What's takin' ya all the way out der?"
"Actually, I'm going there for baseball."
"Aww man! Can I get yer autograph?!"
An eavesdropper behind us springs over my seat. "Sir?! Can I get it too?!"

During a brief layover in Stanfield, Oregon, I exit the mini-mart to find an inebriated woman sitting Indian-style on the sizzling asphalt, waiting to board the bus. Our driver is a rough-around-the-edges type, and is plenty used to playing "good cop-bad cop" in these parts. He opens the conversation by asking, "Ma'am, are you on any medications I should know about, or did ya just drink a little too much?"

I board the bus only to stumble upon an ongoing argument inside. There's an old, homeless, 'I've-done-too-many-drugs-in-my-life' pirate-looking character wearing an eye-patch in a window seat. He's drunk, loud, and irately screaming obscenities to a gentleman standing in the aisle with a young boy:
"Sir, for the last time, you're sitting in my seat."
"Arrrrrgggghhhhhh, I didn't take yer fuc-kin' seat."
"No, my son and I were sitting here. This is our stuff."
"Ahhhhhhhhrrrrrr, fuuuuuck, youuuuu. I found it here

first."

"C'mon, I even left my jacket here. You need to get up and move. These are our seats."

"Ahhhhh, no jacket here! Yerrr makin' up a buncha bulllllllshiiiiiittt!"

"Sir, you're wearing my jacket! Get up, give it, and find another seat!"

"Arrrrrgggghhh, my jacket now! Finderssss keeperssss! Fuuuuccccck Youuuuu!"

There's a brief, tense pause. Then the normal guy loses it. "You betta respect around my kid! Or I'm gonna knock you the fuck out!!"

When we're parked at the bus stop in La Grande, Oregon, a sketchy meth-head starts banging and yelling on the side of the bus. Our driver has the build of a linebacker, and blitzes towards him. Mr. Meth-Head darts like a cheetah, but his sagging pants drop to his ankles as he accelerates. At full speed he trips over himself, bare ass in the air, and face-plants straight into the concrete. *That explains why meth addicts have facial scabs!*

After changing buses in Salt Lake City, the new driver makes the usual, boring announcement, which includes, "There is no smoking on this bus. Smoking cigarettes on this bus is strictly prohibited by federal law." Some smartass redneck in the back yells, "What about smokin' crack!?"

We arrive to Evanston, Wyoming, and the same driver threatens us with a maximum ten-minute break. Twenty minutes later, we're still in our seats waiting to leave. Two frustrated, impatient fellas behind me, from Kentucky and

61

Tennessee, start up the peanut gallery:

> **Kentucky:** "Daayumn man, I could've gone 'n' gotten me a tattoo while we was waitin'."
> **Tennessee:** "All dem folks inside da mini-mart sed dey wanna get'n our bus. Apparently, errrbody on dat bus keeps fightin'."
> **Kentucky:** "Hmm, ya know, I wish dey'd make dem Warheads sour all da way through."
> **Tennessee:** "I been thinkin'. Alan Jackson's pretty coooool, man. He wears boots when he water-skis."

Further down the road, a guy from the front comes back to use the lavatory, and leaves behind an odor that would shame a stink bomb in a cow pasture. Something was already wrong with the sanitation tank, but the problem just worsened by infinity. The toilet won't flush, plus he accidentally left the door open on his way out. Before long, everyone in the back half of the bus, including myself, has their shirt over their noses. We're all in a Greyhound bus, in southern Wyoming, looking like a bunch of Wild West bandits blazing down the Oregon Trail. Kentucky and Tennessee again spark up the peanut gallery:

> **Kentucky:** "Woowww! Der's horse piss, 'n' der's cow piss, but dat shit tops it! If you can't smell dat shit, der's somethin' wrong wit chu!"
> **Tennessee:** "Somebody betta go up der and tell 'em da bathroom's outta order. I can taste dat gag all da way in da back of m'throat!"

A few rows up, an obnoxious little girl bounces in her

seat, pointing and laughing, "Mommy, mommy! If you smelt it, you dealt it!!"

A couple minutes later, the guilty individual comes back down the aisle to make a public announcement. "Boys, I wanna apologize for leavin' the door open like dat. I know it's bad, cuz I can sniff my drift all the way up in da front."

Not long after, an oblivious young boy wakes up from a nap and walks back to use the lavatory. He's maybe seven years old. As he approaches, Kentucky sticks his giant arm out, blocking the boy in the aisle. Kentucky looks him straight in the eye, dead serious, and says, "Listen kid, shitter's outta order. Go back up front and sit yer ass down."

Finally, we make it to Fort Collins, Colorado. It's our last stop before Denver. A woman boards, reeking of smoke, and sits down in the empty seat next to me. She looks like she has been tweaking since the moment she was conceived. As we drive the last hour to Denver, she experiences a terrible onset of withdrawals. Her hands shake while she mumbles gibberish. I ignore her as long as I can. Then, out of the corner of my eye, I mistake it for a Popsicle. I turn my head to see the crazy cat lady gnawing and chewing on a dry cigarette, sucking out all of the tobacco she can get in between her rotting teeth. It's the most depressing and disgusting sight I've ever witnessed.

I'll just go ahead and say it – Worst. Bus. Ever.

Beer guzzling at Coors Field was in full force after thirty straight hours on the bus. I went to the game with my college friend Tom (top left) along with Kristen, Amie, and Claire (bottom).

The amazing Rocky Dog.

Game 8: Coors Field, Denver, CO
July 13, 2012 – Phillies 2, Rockies 6

Category	Rank	Comments
Best Design	11	The boulders, pine trees, and waterfalls behind the center field fence model the Rocky Mountains.
Best View	7	The Colorado sunset can be glorious, especially over the Rockies in the distance.
Best Hot Dog	4	The $6.25 Rocky Dog is one of the best in baseball – foot-long grilled hot dog layered in sautéed bell peppers and onions.
Best Mascot	14	*Dinger* the Dinosaur gets a lot of TV time on the local FSN Rocky Mountain station.
Best Fans	21	In Denver, it's just a bunch of fun people consuming cold beers and long home runs.
Best-Looking Females	7	Talent. After the game, do NOT skip the bars on nearby Larimer Street and Market Street.
Best Entertainment	24	The Rockpile seating section is cheap and entertaining. Grab a Coors, or six.
Best Tradition	17	The reputation as a home-run friendly park. Mile high = low air density = more home runs.
Best Feature	17	The purple seats across the 20th row of upper deck mark the mile-high elevation line.
Final Rank	14th	Stunning, vibrant, and energetic location with babes and beers flowing. Beware: The mile high hangover is awful.

CHAPTER 12
City of Fountains

In Kansas City, baseball is like barbecue sauce; it's in the roots of the culture and holds a special place in the heart of the city. Prior to breaking the Major League color barrier with the Brooklyn Dodgers, Jackie Robinson played for the Kansas City Monarchs, which was the longest-operating franchise of the Negro League[9] era. Surprisingly, though, the Negro League actually had a color barrier of its own. Written and copyrighted by Chuck Brodsky (BMI), this is *The Ballad Of Eddie Klepp*:

The war had finally ended and America had changed
It had beaten back the Nazis but the Jim Crow laws remained
There was talk of staging marches & talk of civil rights
There was talk about a Negro playing baseball with the Whites

He walked into the clubhouse and the card players quit playing
Everybody stopped in the middle of whatever they were saying
It was just like when the sheriff walks into the saloon
He said, "My name is Eddie," as he looked around the room

"This man's here to play baseball," the manager said to the team
"We're all gonna have to live with this…aw, that's not what I mean…

---

[9] The Negro Leagues Baseball Museum is located in Kansas City, Missouri.

You know what I mean" – and they all did…it went without saying
The card players looked at their hands and they went on with their playing

They ran him off the field before a game in Birmingham one night
Made him sit up in the grandstand in the section marked "For Whites"
In his Cleveland Buckeyes uniform, it was a new twist on the law
The marshalls kept their eyes on him and the hecklers ate him raw

Eddie Klepp, he should've run the bases in reverse
A White man in the Negro Leagues, that had to be a first
He could not ride the same busses, or stay in the same motels
He could not eat in the same restaurants, you couldn't have mixed clientele

So while Jackie played for Brooklyn and wore the Dodger Blue
Eddie crossed the color line, the one without a queue
A White man in the Negro Leagues, might as well have been a Jew
Now you mention the name of Eddie Klepp and most everyone says, "Who?"

Holding more notoriety in Negro League history than the irrelevant Eddie Klepp, however, is the success and colorful career of Satchel Paige. Paige was a perennial Negro League All-Star who played the longest tenure of his career with the Kansas City Monarchs (1935 & 1939–1947), and led them to the 1942 Negro League World Series title.

On July 9, 1948, at forty-two years old, Satchel Paige became the oldest player to ever debut in Major League Baseball. He was the first African-American player to appear in the World Series when his Cleveland Indians won it the same year. Despite his age, Paige went on to become a two-time Major League All-Star, and was the first Negro League player inducted into the Baseball Hall of Fame.

In 1965, Kansas City A's owner Charles O. Finley signed fifty-nine-year-old Paige for one game. On the twenty-fifth of September, he pitched three scoreless innings against the Boston Red Sox, fittingly ending his career in Kansas City.

As planned by the team, Paige took the mound again in the fourth inning, but was immediately removed to an overwhelming curtain call at Municipal Stadium. The lights were shut off, matches and cigarette lighters were lit, and the entire crowd sang "The Old Gray Mare" in a standing ovation. Satchel Paige would remain in Kansas City for the rest of his life until he passed away in 1982.

The A's had moved to Kansas City prior to the 1955 season. They originally started in Philadelphia, where they were one of the eight original franchises of the American League. The name "A's" comes from "Athletics", which references the athletic clubs that were popular during the late-1800's. The team's gothic script "A" logo is a trademark originating from the Philadelphia Athletics baseball club. As owner, Connie Mack also managed the Philadelphia A's for their first fifty years, winning five World Series between 1901–1950 with players such as Jimmie Foxx and Lefty Grove.

Connie Mack (actual name: Cornelius McGillicuddy, Sr. – what a classic!) sold the team following the 1954 season to Arnold Johnson, who moved the A's to Kansas City in 1955. Businessman Charlie O. Finley then bought a majority share of the team prior to 1961, and later implemented white cleats instead of black ones. He was also responsible for changing the team's colors to Kelly Green, Gold, and White. Despite the measure of reform he brought to the organization, he again moved the A's in 1968 to their current home in Oakland.

Kansas City went without baseball for just one year before Ewing Kauffman formed an expansion team in 1969. Part of the challenge was naming the franchise, and Kauffman encouraged submissions from the community. A suggestion was entered for the name "Royals", a tribute to the American Royal rodeo, livestock, and horse show held annually in Kansas

City since 1899. "Royals" also followed tradition in the city, holding the same theme as the Monarchs of the Negro League. Historically, other franchises in Kansas City have hierarchal names as well, such as the Kansas City Chiefs of the NFL, and the NBA's Kansas City Kings, which moved to Sacramento in 1985.

Kauffman Stadium is the only ballpark in the American League named in honor of a person, and I can't wait to get there when I arrive to the City of Fountains on Sunday morning, July the fifteenth. Not only does the ballpark share my last name, but the 2012 All-Star Game was played here just five days ago. As I get in line with a family friend to buy tickets, I feel a friendly tap on my shoulder. I'm surprised when I turn to face two women whom I've never met before.

"Hi, do you guys need tickets? Our husbands went golfing today, and we have two extras. They're great seats, right behind home plate…"

And just like that, my ticket luck began.

Me and Billy (formerly of San Diego), who apparently shares my belief that baseball is paradise.

A view of Kauffman Stadium from behind the fountains in right field.

Game 9: Kauffman Stadium, Kansas City, MO
July 15, 2012 – White Sox 2, Royals 1

Category	Rank	Comments
Best Design	13	The baseball-only design incorporates features from Dodger and Angel Stadium.
Best View	18	Simple: Missouri hills and I-70.
Best Hot Dog	6	The $5.00 "Hot Dog" is toasted, hot, and loaded with jalapenos and sauerkraut. It's really good.
Best Mascot	3	*Sluggerrr* is a royal lion, and fires out hot dogs with an air canon gun, usually in the third inning.
Best Fans	19	The booing towards Robinson Cano at the 2012 Home Run Derby was loud and indicative of their passion. The captain left Kansas City slugger Billy Butler off of the American League squad.
Best-Looking Females	15	They're as sweet as that baby-back BBQ sauce, but sometimes ribs are too beefy.
Entertainment	6	Here's a scoreboard joke from Kansas City: "Two guys walk into a bar... The third one ducks."
Best Tradition	22	Garth Brooks' *I've Got Friends In Low Places* plays in the middle of the sixth inning.
Best Feature	11	The multi-level pool of geyser fountains behind right field is the attractive, signature feature at Kauffman Stadium.
Cumulative Rank	10th	An entertaining and intimate ballpark, with geyser-like fountains in right field. An impressive yet simple baseball venue.

CHAPTER 13
Land of 10,000 Couchsurfers

Couchsurfing.org is an online community that offers free networking and hospitality exchanges for the travel community. There are millions of Couchsurfing members in over 250 states and territories around the globe. When members are ready to travel, they can customize their destination and send "couch requests" to other members living in a specific place. When a member is not traveling, they have the option of hosting other Couchsurfing travelers in their home. After meeting, hosting, or surfing, each member writes a reference and categorizes their experience with the other party as positive, neutral, or negative. These references are permanent, and are publicly visible to all Couchsurfing users. It's designed to be a positive, reliable, and fun hospitality site, enabling backpackers to stay, or surf, on couches around the world for free.

A week ago, I reached out to a couple of friends in the Minneapolis area, but found out they would both be out of town during the dates of my visit. Similar to my cycling trip, I've committed to a "no-hotel" rule for the duration of my journey, both to minimize costs and to challenge myself. Without alternative options, I login to Couchsurfing two days before my arrival to Minneapolis and post an "open" couch request in the area. Rather than reaching out to multiple individuals, this option allows potential hosts the opportunity to contact me first (which saves me both time and effort while allowing me to be selective). Within an hour of posting, I receive an exciting, unexpected response:

> *Hey Cody, have you found a host yet? I see that you're coming awfully soon. I can certainly give you a place to crash if you still need one, though I've got a gig rehearsal 7:30-9:30, so I wouldn't be able to catch the game.* **Oddly, though, I'm hosting a pair of surfers tomorrow night who are ALSO traveling to see all of the 30 MLB stadiums.** *I don't know what their plans are, but maybe you're going to the same game. I'll check with them too. Happy traveling, Ross*

Without hesitation, I eagerly accept Ross's offer. The next day, he sends me a text:

> **Ross:** *I'm with my other MLB surfers and they want to meet up with you. Do you mind if I give them your number?*
> **Me:** *Of course you can! Did they already go to the Twins game?*
> **Ross:** *No, they're going tomorrow. You could go with them.*

The next day, while riding the bus through the cornfields of Iowa (near the Field of Dreams) on my way to Minneapolis, I receive a text from an unknown number:

> **(717):** *Hey Cody! This is Emily - Ross gave us your number. We're going to Sneaky Pete's before the game tonight. If you can, come meet up with us!*

Me: *Hey Emily, sounds good - My bus arrives at 5:30, and I'll cruise over.*

Target Field is within walking distance of the Minneapolis Greyhound station, but Ross has offered to come pick up my oversized bag, which is too large to bring inside the stadium. It also gives Ross and I a few minutes to get acquainted with each other, so he doesn't have to welcome a total stranger to his apartment in the middle of the night. Ross is a tall, lanky, fourth-year at the University of Minnesota. As expected, he's an awesome guy, and drops me off at Sneaky Pete's on his way to band practice.

I show my I.D. at the door and walk inside the bar. Immediately, I come across yet another tall, lanky man, but fifty years my elder. He's standing on a short stool behind a table with a small cashbox. In front of the stand is an aluminum ice tub filled with $4.00 tallboys, the gameday special. I give him five dollars as he cracks open my beer, and I then start looking for these other MLB surfers.

An immediate bond is formed once I track down Emily and her friend Colin. The odds of bumping into random strangers on the same ballpark pilgrimage are relatively small, so it feels like I've discovered two long lost cousins in the middle of nowhere. Before we dive into trip comparisons, Colin asks, "You know who you bought that beer from, don't you?" I look at him, and shake my head. "No, not at all."

"Dude, that's Wally The Beerman!"

As it turns out, Wally The Beerman is the most famous beer vendor in the country. For forty-one years, he climbed the stairs at both the Metrodome and Target Field shouting his signature "Cold beer here!" He has built a cult-like following that has inspired the production of "Wally The Beerman" posters, trading cards, and even bobblehead dolls. But on September 30, 2010, Wally and seven other vendors were cited for selling alcohol to minors during an undercover sting operation at Target Field. Although Wally was acquitted in March 2011, his career inside Minneapolis sports venues came to an abrupt end. Alternatively, he accepted a celebrity gig at Sneaky Pete's, where today, he sells beer before-and-after every Twins game.

After Colin, Emily, and I crush our beers together, we walk down the street to Target Field, which is beautifully constructed on the north side of downtown. In our seats halfway through the game, I'm still trying to figure out how Colin and Emily know each other. I've figured out that they're not a couple, but I'm left wondering how they wound up with each other on a road trip around the country. I can't even imagine what their conversations are like during long hours in the car. Then, a little while later, the Kiss Cam appears on the scoreboard.

Colin (jokingly): "Emily, if you and I get on the Kiss Cam, I'm gonna make out with you super hard."

Emily: "You touch me… and I'll punch you straight in the face."

After three hours and twenty-two minutes of baseball resulting in a 19-7 Twins victory, Colin and Emily drive to Milwaukee. I bid them farewell and head to Ross's apartment, unsure if I'll ever see them again.

MAKING TECHNOLOGY **WORK FOR YOU**

Me, Colin, Emily, and some random guy whose name I have forgotten, at the Best Buy photo booth inside Target Field.

My Minnesota Twins Budweiser can served by Wally The Beerman at Sneaky Pete's.

Game 10: Target Field, Minneapolis, MN
July 16, 2012 – Orioles 7, Twins 19

Category	Rank	Comments
Best Design	8	Target Field is beautifully confined in a fantastic cityscape. The vertical construction gives a unique feel.
Best View	8	The Minneapolis skyline looms overhead, providing one of the best downtown views in the country.
Best Hot Dog	16	Original Twins Dog is $4.00, but Monday is $1.00 hot dog night. I like $1.00.
Best Mascot	11	*TC the Bear* gets the fans all riled up.
Best Fans	16	They're just happy to be outdoors during the summer.
Best-Looking Females	1	These tundra foxes must hibernate in the winter, and wear mini-skirts all summer. I felt like the big bad wolf.
Best Entertainment	13	If you go to a Twins game, chances are you'll see a dance-off between fans on top of the dugouts.
Best Tradition	26	End of the eighth inning is *Journey's* "Don't Stop Believin'." Good song, unoriginal idea.
Best Feature	20	The light-up home run feature above center field is shaped as the state of Minnesota.
Final Rank	13th	Target Field is a premiere, state-of-the-art, underrated downtown ballpark with a unique design. They did everything right.

CHAPTER 14
Brew Town

Diehard Brewers fan Amy Williams is a "hot" topic in Milwaukee. "Front Row Amy" has become a mini-celebrity by establishing herself as the highly-attractive wife and mom who attends a majority of Brewers home games, alone. Since 2010, her season ticket seat has been directly behind home plate in the front row, within the frame of every pitch on TV. Adding to the peculiarity, she manually keeps score throughout each game and never misses a pitch, a quality that impresses both neighboring fans and viewers at home.

So who is Front Row Amy? That's what this morning's feature article in the Milwaukee Sentinel-Journal seeks to answer. I'm sitting at a table at Broken Yolk Sandwich Shoppe on Wisconsin Avenue, two blocks west of Marquette University. It's a few minutes past ten-o'clock this morning, and my breakfast bagel is digesting happily in my stomach. Meanwhile, my nose is buried in the paper.

Suddenly, I hear a honk outside. I set the newspaper down, wave goodbye to my cashier, and exit the café. When I reach the curb, I open the rear door of a silver sedan and crawl inside.

It took only thirty-six hours for us to reunite. Emily

navigates while Colin drives, and we make the short drive to the Miller Brewing Factory. Two Guys, A Girl, And A Brewery.

By noon, after a tour and three beers, I feel fantastic as we leave Miller Valley. Colin and Emily went to the Brewers game last night, but have offered to drop me off at Miller Park for this afternoon's game on their way to Chicago. When we arrive to the outskirts of the parking lot, I wish them the best as their adventure continues. I grab my glove, my daypack, and bid them farewell for the second time in three days.

Feeling tipsy, warm, and excited for baseball, I happily bound through the midday tailgate festivities at Miller Park. It's a beautiful Wednesday in mid-July, and the Brewers faithful are out in full force. The RV lot on the east side of the stadium is packed with rowdy Bavarian descendants tossing back beers by the boot. It feels like a playoff atmosphere, and it pretty much is, I suppose, whenever the St. Louis Cardinals are in town.

I'm one hundred meters from the entrance gate when I hear a friendly, inquisitive voice vying for my attention. "You planning on catching a foul ball today?" I hear a woman ask. I immediately look her way, wondering if it might be Front Row Amy. The woman smiles, beer in hand, wearing white pants and a blue Brewers jersey. She's dedicated to winning, but it's definitely not Front Row Amy. Nonetheless, I'm excited to talk to a stranger.

"Yep, and when I do, I'm gonna give it to you," I teasingly respond. I *love* making new friends, and it's pretty easy to do when everyone is boozing in a parking lot on a Wednesday afternoon.

"Not many people bring their mitt these days," she says, referencing the glove in my hand.

"And not many people catch foul balls," I playfully

react. "Today might be my lucky day."

I launch into my background story, explaining my ballpark trip and my plan to write a book. After I formally introduce myself, she reaches into her purse and hands me a lukewarm beer. "Cody, welcome to Wisconsin," she says. "I'm Connie."

Connie and I approach the entrance to Miller Park while I chug my Miller Lite. As we wrap up our conversation, we say goodbye as I head towards the ticket window. I haven't taken two steps when she stops me dead in my tracks with an incredible offer.

"I completely forgot!" she exclaims. "My son's girlfriend got a bladder infection and couldn't come today! We have an extra ticket!"

"Really?" Sounds amazing!" I respond, cracking up at her explanation. *Too much information.*

Fast forwarding, our seats turn out to be fantastic – field level behind the third base dugout. Throughout the game, Connie's husband Rob and their son Damien share insightful knowledge about baseball in Milwaukee. In the late innings, my impending sobriety reminds me of my proximity to Front Row Amy. A few sections to my right, as advertised, she's in the front row directly behind home plate.

After the game, I get in touch with Front Row Amy, popularly followed on her Twitter profile @BrewerGirl823. She agreed to an exclusive interview for this book:

Do you have any game day rituals or superstitions? If so, do you mind sharing them?
"I don't have any game day rituals, but I do follow the same routine every time I go to Miller Park. I go in the front entrance,

81

head to the bathroom (it's a long drive), go to my seat, attach my Brewers seat cushion, get out my water or Diet Mountain Dew, choose a pencil (there's a superstition – lucky pencil!), and fill out the lineups in my scorebook. I always draw a little heart by Corey Hart's name, and write "Sugar" for Segura (my one nickname for a player). I never wear Brewers shirts or hats because the team has lost EVERY time I've worn Brewers gear, no exaggeration here, EVERY time. Though I've been thinking this year I might try wearing a Brewers shirt to a game to see what happens. Oh! And I have a few pairs of lucky boots and shoes."

What's the most important thing you've missed to attend a Brewers game?

"I've never missed anything important to go to a Brewers game. I go to about forty games a year. I choose the ones I will attend in February and schedule them around important family events. Once in a while, there's a surprise game if I don't sell my ticket, but I'll only go if there are no family events going on. One of those "surprise" games was Trevor Hoffman's 600th save! And if a family emergency comes up and I'm supposed to go to a game, I'll sell my ticket. Family comes first. My haters don't believe that, but what do they know? Nothing. I'm home ALL THE TIME in the offseason. I work from home, I'm there when my kids get home from school, I make dinner, do laundry, all that fun stuff. And during the season, I'm home with my family all day and a lot of evenings. I'm home MOST of the time. Plus, when I'm at the game, my family can see me on TV! I believe it's very important for mothers to have something that is their own. A passion. An escape. Mine is Brewers baseball."

You put a huge smile on my face with the Trevor Hoffman reference. Are your friends and family supportive of your role as "Front Row Amy?" Do they ever come to the game with you?

"My husband comes to a few games with me and we sit in loge on the second level. My family is very supportive of me. They do miss me during the season – though I am home most of the time – but they think it's awesome that I'm doing something that I love and that makes me happy. My good friends are supportive. I've definitely discovered who my REAL friends are over the past couple seasons."

How long do you plan on continuing your role as "Front Row Amy"?

I plan to keep my seat forever! "Front Row Amy" was created by people watching the game, so I guess it's up to them how long it continues. Probably no one will be interested in me anymore when I'm eighty.

Manually keeping score has become sort of an ancient art – Why do you do it?

I keep score because I absolutely LOVE doing it! It keeps me very focused on the game, on every single pitch. And it makes me feel like I'm part of the game.

Did you grow up in the Milwaukee area? Are you a lifelong Brewers fan, or is it something you came into as an adult?

I was born in Evanston, Illinois and lived there until I was nine years old when my mother and I moved to Oshkosh, Wisconsin. I didn't begin watching Brewers baseball until 2007. Some people fault me for that, saying I'm not a real Brewers fan because I haven't loved them my whole life. But I was just never exposed to baseball before 2007. My mom and dad got divorced when I was two years old, so dad wasn't around to play catch with me or take me to games, and neither my mom nor my dad were huge baseball fans. In May 2007, I saw an article about the Brewers on the front page of the sports section of the Oshkosh Northwestern, which said that the Brewers were in first place and a very exciting team. There was also a big picture of JJ Hardy in that article which may or may not have influenced my decision to watch. I watched my first Brewers game the night I read the article and fell in love! Really! It was an instant attraction to the team – both their enthusiasm and personality – and the game of baseball. From that night on I watched as many games as I could and visited Miller Park for the first time not long after.

Was it hard for you to obtain season tickets directly behind home plate?

It was not difficult to get my seat behind home plate when I bought it. It's a single seat – the four seats to my left and right are owned by season ticket holders. Most people don't want to go to games by themselves, so it had been available for years. I actually sat there for a couple games in 2008. I'll never forget the first time I sat in that front row seat. It's awe-inspiring to sit there. You're right down on the field! With no heads blocking your view! It's so amazing. I wish every Brewers fan could experience it. I already owned two seats in the fourth row of that section, but went to a lot of games by myself. The decision to let go of my two seats and buy the one was not easy. I wasn't sure I'd be able to sell a single seat for games I didn't go to. I wasn't sure if I wanted to be on TV because I get a little crazy at games. But in the end, after many discussions with family and friends, I decided to buy the front row seat and give up my two seats in the fourth row. I bought my seat before the 2010 season, and if I had waited another year, it probably wouldn't have been available.

I love the Bratwurst at Miller Park. Do you have a favorite food item at Brewers games?

Actually I don't eat when I go to games! When I'm happy and excited, as I always am when I go to Miller Park, I'm just not hungry.

Lastly, what is your favorite thing about being Front Row Amy?

My favorite thing about being Front Row Amy is that I get to meet people that I wouldn't ordinarily get to meet. I met Tom Haudricourt and Todd Rosiak last season, two Brewers beat reporters who I admire very much. I met a lot of the T-Rats (Brewers single-A affiliate) last season as well. Also, it's very cool that the team and staff at Miller Park know who I am now. Makes me feel like part of the team. Since I began watching the Brewers in 2007 it's been a big dream of mine...to be part of the team in some way. But I never thought sitting in the best seat in the house and doing what I love to do, watching the Brewers and keeping score, would help that dream become realized.

Me (glove in hand), Connie, Rob, and Damien sitting behind the third base dugout at Miller Park.

Me, Colin, and Emily (left to right) having fun at the Miller Brewing Factory before the game.

Game 11: Miller Park, Milwaukee, WI
July 18, 2012 – Cardinals 3, Brewers 4

Category	Rank	Comments
Best Design	17	Miller Park features a fan-shaped convertible roof and huge glass panels bringing in exterior light.
Best View	26	Fairly enclosed, but the open roof brings much desired sunlight in the summer months.
Best Hot Dog	5	The $4.50 Bratwurst is amazing. Keep an eye out for the "Special Stadium Sauce."
Best Mascot	5	*Bernie The Brewer* has his own clubhouse and home run slide high above the left field seats.
Best Fans	5	Beers and brats in German country = rowdy. Over 37,000 passionate fans for a mid-July day game.
Best-Looking Females	20	Front Row Amy (@BrewerGirl823 on Twitter) certainly helps the cause.
Best Entertainment	5	After the Seventh Inning Stretch, fans sing "Roll Out The Barrel" to honor the local beer-making history.
Best Tradition	5	Mascot races originated in Milwaukee with the famous Sausage Race.
Best Feature	5	Above left field, *Bernie The Brewer* barrels down his spiraling slide after each HR.
Final Rank	2nd	I'm shocked how many "5's" it got. That's strictly coincidental, but the high ranking isn't.

CHAPTER 15
Windy City, Part I

In Chicago, I stayed with my friend Mikey for six nights. He's the guy who flew all the way to Miami when I got back from South America. Yeah, the one who *loves* baseball. Anyway, this chapter is a little bit different from the rest, and that's because I didn't write it. Mikey did. Since there are two teams in Chicago, and room for two chapters, I asked Mikey to shed some light on my visit from his perspective. This is what he provided, straight from the horse's mouth:

"Why would I bring a suitcase when all of my stuff fits in a backpack?" Cody responded, dumbfounded, as I searched for his supplemental luggage vessel. I had a confused look on my face, not fully understanding how he could be making this voyage with a glorified school bag.

I've backpacked through Europe, wandered the Gringo Trail in South America, and camped several weekends away, but I have never met a soul who travels, better yet adventures, with less personal property than Cody Kaufman. Where you or I might be proud to fly home for the holidays with a suitcase that fits in an overhead compartment, Cody doesn't need more than a fanny-pack and the clothes on his back.

Anyway, when he arrived to town, I met him on the corner of

Belmont and Broadway in the Lakeview neighborhood of Chicago. After he convinced me that he wasn't wearing an invisibility cloak covering another bag somewhere, we started the stroll back to my apartment just a couple blocks away. He was exhausted after an intense bout through several cities and stadiums, something like four in three days. I could be exaggerating, but I wouldn't put it past him. He was here to stay, at least a relatively longer respite than he had had in a while.

Did I mention Cody and I are like best friends? Well, we are. And did I mention I was going through a rough patch with my now ex-girlfriend? Well, we were. Nothing like having a good friend around when all you want to do is forgot about your stupid problems. The first night started off pretty slow, and by that I mean, we each had about eight Fireball shots at the bar.

If you're familiar with a vagabond's habits, then you might understand the frequency in which one enjoys Subway. The five-dollar footlong can really appease any traveler's taste buds, or at least keep a stomach such as Cody's from growling for an hour or two. Upon arrival, he was even so happy to show me his coupon for a two-for-one. WOW! Jackpot. After Cody went to the Cubs game the following day, he decided to redeem his pot-o'-gold on his way back to my apartment. Like any good friend, he texted me as I got off work, telling me dinner was on his dime. What a gentleman. I arrived home soon thereafter, craving my footlong turkey on wheat, with no olives and honey mustard, and found that Cody had already plowed through his entire sandwich. Probably took him two bites. As I plopped down next to him, he started into his story. And if you haven't heard a Cody Kaufman story, just know that David Blaine couldn't hold his breath for the entire thing. For your sake, I will summarize.

Cody walks into Subway happy as a clam, ready to order his two sandwiches while fondling the coupon in his pocket like it's The Ring. After getting "the works", he stops at the register and holds out the magic coupon, waiting for his massive discount. The manager examines the

WINDY CITY, PART I

coupon and plugs in, as Cody put it, "some bullshit numbers", and the total comes out to twelve bucks. How could that be? He had a two-for-one coupon! So the exchange commences with Cody stating that the coupon promises a free sandwich "of equal or less value" as long as he purchases a drink with the first one. But the manager claims he's required to buy two sodas, one for each sandwich. Cody doesn't want soda, so there's a major conflict of interest. On top of that, the manager pulls a fast one by ringing him up for two 6-inch subs instead of one footlong, which, as any Subway connoisseur knows, is more expensive. Cody's not having it, because Cody didn't order four 6-inch subs, he ordered two footlongs, and his magic coupon says he gets a massive discount on the second one. This four-for-two deal is the product of a scam artist, and Cody calls the manager out on it. It becomes a Mexican standoff. Also not having it are the people waiting in line. Cody threatens to walk out, but he also knows he needs those sandwiches. After all, one of them is for me. In the end, unlike most days, Cody walks out of Subway dejected, with two more sodas than he ever wanted, four 6-inch subs, and five less greenbacks. He's pissed, but I can't imagine how much worse it might've been if he didn't get to charge it to his Subway gift card. "It's not the money," he reiterated, "It's the principle. Don't ever go to the Subway by Wrigley Field."

Blah, blah, blah, whatever you say buddy. It's the weekend now and poor me has just been notified that his girlfriend would like a break. After pretending to be okay with that turn of events, I held a reciprocal venting session with Cody (a.k.a. Mr. Rational slash "your problems are futile, stop caring so much"), which honestly, always makes me feel better.

The weekend had arrived! We were going big. Especially me, since it's a proven fact you can drink your problems away. And big we went... errr, I think we went. I really don't remember.

As I stumbled out of bed the next morning, I made a soft "Cody" moan that a dog would have had trouble hearing. I figured he was still sleeping on the couch, so I went about my morning ritual. As I sat down on the toilet, I opened my phone to piece together the previous night.

"WHAT THE F#&%?" I had a dozen texts and calls from him, spanning between 2:00am and twenty minutes ago. *Shit, shit, SHIT.* It wasn't until I read through his texts and listened to his voicemails that I realized he had found a comfortable bed in a park bush on the *SOUTH SIDE OF CHICAGO!*

Although I have slept unusually comfortable in a bed of foliage in the past, this slightly worried me. Cody had slept in a random park clear on the other side of town, and even worse, on the South Side, where us uptight yuppie Lakeviewers dare not venture. What kind of a friend was I? When I called him back, he said he was still unsure how he got there. He was hungry (which is a vital sign from him), and quickly on the move like Jason Bourne. I told him to figure it out, fast.

Before I go any further, I am going to Quentin Tarantino this plot and rewind to the night before. We had eight-o'clock dinner reservations with my friends Amy, Morgan, and Ivan. This included several pitchers of margaritas before we went to a bar. Then, later that night, we went to another bar, I think, and then... honestly, no idea.

Baffled as to how Cody wound up in this fabulous arrangement, I call Amy and Morgan to ask them what happened. They tell me that Cody cabbed me home at some point, and then cabbed back out to meet up with them. They all went to one more bar, and then to a club downtown. By the end of the night, they had lost him, and just figured he had made his way back to my apartment. That clearly never happened.

The girls proceed to lash me for being so irresponsible, further complicating the position I put my friend in. I'm even more upset that I missed all of his calls, but I also know that a howler monkey, let alone a ring tone, couldn't have woken me from my inebriated slumber. I try to soothe their glaring concern by informing them that Cody is alive, and... well, I think he's alive. Why or how he ended up thirteen miles from my house was mind-boggling and not worth the strain on my pounding skull. I can't deal with this, so I hang up with them.

An hour on the clock ticks by as I anxiously await the return of *my houseguest. He doesn't show. So I call him again. No answer.*

Okay, what the hell is going on? Did he get jumped on his journey north? Hop on the wrong train? Go back to Subway to fight the manager?

Another thirty minutes passes by. I am really freaking out.

Worried and sweating Jameson and gingers, I then hear the ding of a bell, not from my door, but from my iPhone. I look down and see that Cody has sent me a text message. Thank God, finally. Very simply, though, it reads:

> *Hey, just so you know: Amy, Morgan and I have been pranking you all morning. I stayed with them last night, and we're out apartment shopping.*

Dicks.

I thought this was the Cubs mascot, but I later found out they don't have one. This unauthorized phony (Billy Cub) actually tried to get a tip out of me. The Cubs eventually banned him from Wrigley Field on July 20, 2013.

Game 12: Wrigley Field, Chicago, IL
July 19, 2012 – Marlins 2, Cubs 4

Category	Rank	Comments
Best Design	9	The manual scoreboard, obstructive beams, and ancient speakers testify that Wrigley is the second oldest ballpark in baseball.
Best View	11	Looking out to the northeast is a view of the Wrigley rooftops and Lake Michigan.
Best Hot Dog	12	The $6.00 Chicago Dog is grilled-to-order with sautéed onions, diced tomatoes, and peperoncinis.
Best Mascot	28	Though a young bear cub appears on the logo, the Cubs don't have an official team mascot.
Best Fans	4	Home to the Bleacher Bums, Cubs fans are talkative, proud, come early, and stay late.
Best-Looking Females	10	Good-looking, fun, and slightly above average.
Best Entertainment	9	Cubs brass band and other musical tributes, such as "Go, Cubs, Go" after each home win.
Best Tradition	3	"Take Me Out To The Ballgame" (R.I.P. Harry Caray) is the seventh-inning staple notoriously famous at Wrigley Field.
Best Feature	14	The red brick outfield wall is a classic Wrigley icon covered in ivy plants.
Final Rank	5th	Wrigley Field is an old-time baseball Mecca with diehard fans, culture, and tradition.

CHAPTER 16
Windy City, Part II

Mikey and his roommate Neal are high school friends from Orange County. Neal actually grew up in Chicago, but his family moved to Southern California several years before he attended U.C. Santa Cruz. After college, Neal moved back to Chi-Town, and Mikey joined him a couple years later.

This Neal character, who I had never met before I arrived, is in love with my baseball tour as much as I am. Since I've been here, he has been obsessively consumed with showing me the proper Chicago experience. Steadfast and dedicated, his efforts include educating me about everything between restaurants, baseball history, and Chicago culture. He has already made a valiant attempt to take me to every iconic sausage joint in the city, and when it's not that, it has been a quest for Chicago-style deep-dish pizza. After a weekend of pure eating and drinking, I express to him that, "The only thing people do here is eat, and drink." He responds, "You think that now? You should come back in the winter."

On Monday morning, while everyone is working, Neal suggests that I borrow Mikey's bike to go visit the world famous Billy Goat Tavern, which was established in 1934 by Billy Sianis, the same guy who placed the *Curse of the Billy Goat* on the Cubs during the 1945 World Series. In an effort to sweat out the weekend booze, I take myself on a ten-mile tour around the Windy City, which is extremely hot and sticky on this particular day. By early afternoon I'm hungry, dehydrated, and more than ready for my pit stop at the Billy Goat.

Billy Goat Tavern is a hole-in-the-wall joint that's located in a dark corner next to the Chicago River underneath the Michigan Avenue Bridge. Its infamy inspired a popular Saturday Night Live skit in 1978 that featured Bill Murray, Dan Aykroyd, John Belushi, and Loraine Newman. As I walk through the door and down the steps, I enter a place that for decades has been frozen in time.

"Hey kid, whatd'ya want? Double Cheezeborger?" shouts the man behind the counter.

I'm barely through the door and down the steps. "Gimme a minute," I respond, feeling like Michael J. Fox in *Back to the Future*.

The vinyl stools are easily sixty years old. The original wood walls are covered with black-and-white framed photographs and news clippings. It's like an antique shack full of mid-century memorabilia.

"So? What's it gonna be?" the man intervenes. "Double cheezeborger?" He's making it real clear that their ranting reputation is no joke.

"Hold on," I insist. I walk around the counter to examine the menu.

"Same menu – both sides! Double cheezeborger's the best we got!" he pipes. I ignore him and continue looking. "Don't look at the menu," he exclaims, "Go with the cheezeborger!"

"I'm thinking one of the sandwiches might be good..." I ponder out loud.

"Listen kid, I work here, you don't. I order, not you. Double cheez!"

At this point, Dr. Wisecrack has me unnerved, but I'm still undecided. "Hmm, I'm still looking it over," I tease him, referring to the menu.

"No menu here! We serve cheezeborgers! No fries – cheeps! No Pepsi – Coke!" His beady brown eyes lock into mine.

"Okay, uhh, hold on…" I insist.

"The double cheezeborger's the best we got! Ain't nothin' betta!" he impatiently exclaims.

I'm the only person in line, but this guy is going to have a conniption if I don't order the double cheeseBURGER. The cashier gal, smacking her gum, joins in the stare down. They're ganging up on me like they're the Chicago cheezeborger mafia.

I decide to test their Chicago blood and push them a bit further. "How's the pastrami sandwich?" I inquire.

"No!!! No pastrami sandwich!! Double cheezeborger!! The best we got! No fries - cheeps! No Pepsi - Coke!"

"Fiiiiiiiiiiiine. I'll go with the double frickin' cheeseBURGER," I conclude.

"Cheeps?!" asks the man.

"No chips."

"But we have no fries," he responds, clearly confused.

"I know. I just don't want chips."

He's perplexed, but moves on. "No Pepsi here – Coke?"

I throw him a curveball. "Sprite."

As I chomp into my double cheezeborger, sweat continues to bead down my forehead after my ride around the city. I watch an episode of Jeopardy on the ancient tube TV, and then prepare for my exit. I make one last stop at the

97

counter, and politely ask the man for a refill of water. He points due south, directly across the street, and responds, "Hey kid! Go fill 'er up in the riva!"

The next night, Mikey, Neal, and I head to U.S. Cellular Field for my thirteenth game of the tour. Neal *loves* his White Sox, so much so that I'm beginning to wonder if he's employed ambassador for the team. Every night while I've been here, he's lured me into another history lesson about South Side Chicago, branding the Sox into my memory. It's like he's sick of the fact that every summer, Chicago attracts out-of-towners who immediately visit Wrigley Field, giving preference to the crosstown Cubbies. The more I listen and learn, the more I realize there's an underlying, intra-city hostility between the Cubs and the White Sox. The masses are biased towards the historic ballpark in Wrigleyville and the chronicled franchise of the Cubs, but of the two teams, it's actually the White Sox who have accomplished the most success. Nonetheless, Sox fans carry a chip on their shoulder like an unruly underdog, possibly attributed to the blue-collar workmanship associated with the south side of town.

On our way home that night following a White Sox win, Neal tells me an animated story that perfectly depicts the deep-seated hostility between Chicago's two teams. He says:

"I'm gonna tell you a little story about baseball in Chicago. When I was in high school, I used to sneak onto this golf course by my house and play the back nine. This one day, I'm behind these three guys, and they holler, 'Hey kid, you wanna join?' So I jump in with these guys and start playing, and we're having a real good time. After the second hole, I'm ridin' in the cart

with one of the guys and he asks, 'You a Cubs fan?'
and I say, 'Nah... Sox fan.' Then, I kid you not, this
guy slams on the brakes, turns to me, and screams, 'A
Sox fan?! Get the fuck outta my cart!!' So yeah, I
ended up walking the rest of the course by myself."

Neal's story confirms the sense I've been feeling all
week. What's difficult to understand, however, is why this
grudge even exists? The White Sox play in the American
League and don't directly compete against the Cubs in the
National League. In fact, until interleague play began in 1997,
it had been ninety-one years since the White Sox and Cubs last
played each other! The previous matchup was in 1906, when
the White Sox beat the Cubs to win the World Series.

I've spent enough time in New York, Los Angeles,
and the San Francisco Bay Area, the only other places with two
baseball teams, to understand that the tension in Chicago is
unique. For over eighty years the Sox played at Comiskey Park,
located near Chicago's historic meatpacking industry and
immigrant communities. Demographically, the residents from
this area are hardworking blue-collar citizens, as opposed to the
white-collar stereotype up north. A week in Chicago isn't
enough to fully comprehend the differentiation, but it seems
that to a certain extent, the rivalry traces back to a segregation
of class lines. The Sox's "South Siders" nickname isn't just a
geographic identity, but a cultural and economic one as well.
Over the course of the last century, the White Sox have
evolved as a symbol of pride in the South Side community, a
devotion that has been passed down through generations as a
nemesis against the Cubbies. And it goes both ways.

Mikey (left) and Neal (right) with me at US Cellular Field. The Chicago skyline looms in the background.

Mikey (left) and I (right) in the bushes during our big night out in Chicago. He was certainly deserving of my prank the next morning.

Game 13: U.S. Cellular Field, Chicago, IL
July 24, 2012 – Twins 4, White Sox 11

Category	Rank	Comments
Best Design	27	Fantastic viewing decks with an attached parking garage and entertainment complex.
Best View	13	Peering north from the upper concourse is an awesome view of the Chicago skyline.
Best Hot Dog	1	For the quality, taste, and price, the $5.25 Polish Sausage is the best thing in baseball.
Best Mascot	24	Is *Southpaw* a dinosaur or a lizard? It just seems weird.
Best Fans	14	White Sox nation vastly carries a blue-collar chip on their shoulder. It seems like everyone in Chicago loves baseball.
Best-Looking Females	28	I saw as many tramp stamp tattoos as I would on the Jerry Springer show. That's not good.
Best Entertainment	28	Besides a kids dance-off, it's pretty basic on the entertainment scale.
Best Tradition	12	The tradition is the South Side – the food, the culture, the history, and how the Sox have stood the test of time.
Best Feature	29	After each home run, fireworks blastoff near the lollipop-like swirly features above center field.
Final Rank	26th	Chicago is known for its meat, and the Polish Sausage alone is worth the visit to "The Cell."

CHAPTER 17
Gateway to the West

As my bus crosses the Mississippi River from Illinois to Missouri, I realize this is my first time to St. Louis in eight years. Rising above the river to my right is the famous St. Louis Arch, nicknamed the Gateway to the West, glimmering amid the downtown skyline in the late afternoon sun. After crossing to the Missouri side, the bus exits the freeway near Busch Stadium, which sits two blocks west of the river in the heart of downtown. The Cardinals host the Dodgers tonight, and first pitch is less than two hours away.

Conveniently, the Greyhound Station is only six blocks from Busch Stadium near the Scottrade Center, home of the NHL's St. Louis Blues. Getting from the bus terminal to the ballpark is as easy as walking east down Clark Avenue. My current problem, though, has nothing to do with transportation.

As I briefly mentioned in Minnesota, my travel backpack is slightly too large for ballpark entry. In other cities, I've had a plan or solution to get around this, but that's not the case today. I've already told my Couchsurfing host that I'm going to ride the MetroLink to his house *after* the game. Besides, it's much too far and too late to go drop off my bag

103

and come back.

A week earlier, when I had arrived to the Greyhound Station in Milwaukee, I had put my bag in storage for the day until I departed for Chicago in the evening. Some Greyhound terminals offer this service, but I quickly find out St. Louis isn't one of them.

Hypothetically, I could postpone the Cardinals game until tomorrow, but that would mean going in the middle of the day. Right now, at 5:30 in the evening, the outside temperature is 105 degrees. 105 degrees sucks anywhere, but let me tell you, it REALLY sucks in St. Louis. There's a snowball's chance in hell I'm signing up for a day game.

Without a plan, my backpack and I trudge towards Busch Stadium in the sweltering humidity. I've been in situations like this before, and I have faith that I'll figure it out. As I get closer to the ballpark, I see fans parking their cars. For a brief second, I actually consider asking some folks if I can store my bag in their vehicle, but I manage to resist the act of desperation. Not only will it make me look like the Unabomber, but it's also too much of a risk. I exercise common sense and move on.

At the corner of Clark and 11th Street, I pull out my iPhone and zoom to my location on the map. I notice a hotel directly across the street from Busch Stadium, which inspires a hopeful idea. I walk three more blocks and enter the driveway of the Westin St. Louis. The valet attendant offers a curious nod as I approach the revolving doors. Through his eyes, he sees a twenty-five year-old wearing fluorescent Nike's and a San Diego Padres hat, carrying a camouflage military pack into an upscale hotel. I know exactly what he's thinking: *Who shows up to the Westin (on foot!) with a military-grade backpack in 105-degree heat? Nobody.* Nonetheless, I grant him a warm greeting as I pass by.

As I go inside, I reflect on my two summers working as a hotel bellhop in Santa Barbara. I understand hotel management, and have a mental advantage recognizing that the staff is programmed to accommodate all requests. With this in mind, I enter the marble lobby with the confidence of a lion. Like I own the place.

In the back of my mind, though, there is still a shadow of doubt that an upscale hotel will hand out a favor to a guy off the street. But that's when I remember... I am Cody Kaufman. I am charming. I have a suave demeanor that people don't deny. I possess the skill set to sell an ice cube to an Eskimo. My personality and intellect are biologically engineered for situations like this. I am in control. I will succeed.

As I march through the grand foyer, a marble wall barricades my view of the front desk. Before I turn the corner, I imagine the ideal employee waiting for me on the other side. In a perfect scenario, it would be a cute, mid-twenties blonde with features that compliment a soft, sweet Midwest personality. There'd be no one else waiting in line, and she'd be alone, ready to assist me with undivided attention.

When I turn the corner and get my first glimpse, I am beside myself. Standing there (waiting for me!) is an extremely cute, mid-twenties blonde, all alone. *Sweet Jesus.* As I move towards her, I walk tall while holding seductive eye contact, pretending that she's walking down the aisle on our wedding day. I notice her nametag: *Katie.*

She welcomes me with a smile. "Hi there, how ya doin' this afternoon?" she inquires on my approach.

"I'm doing great, thanks!" I reinforce convincingly. My sales switch flips on. I lean over the counter, give her a devilish grin, and intimately voice my idea. "Listen, Katie," I begin in a soft tone, "I'm traveling around the country this summer going to all of the baseball stadiums. It's been awesome so far, but I just arrived to St. Louis, and I really need a place to store my bag while I'm at the Cardinals game tonight. I'm not a guest, but would you be willing to help me out?" I give her my best puppy dog stare that I know she can't refuse.

Based on the sweet, hospitable response that ensues, I'm pretty sure Katie would've agreed to anything. I could've pulled a parachute out of my backpack and asked her to base jump off the building with me, and she would've said, "Yes". I could've asked her to take two shots of tequila with me right there on the front desk, and she would've said, "¡Sí chico!" This is why Midwest girls are so wonderful. They say, "Yes!" to everything.

In a matter of fifteen seconds, Katie and I have built an unspoken connection. Instead of the typical, facetious lobby conversation, it feels like we're getting ready to do something illegal at the end of a first date. She's asking all sorts of fun questions while studying my movements, and gladly takes my backpack behind the counter. Rather than storing it in a room or a closet, though, I notice she puts it directly behind her against the wall. "I'm gonna keep it right here," she tells me. "I get off at 11:00. Will you be back by then?"

Without saying a word, I backpedal a few steps, offer a confirming wink, and stride out as confidently as I did on the way in. Mission: Accomplished.

I need a T-shirt that reads, "I Survived Busch Stadium Fever." It was 102 degrees, plus humidity, at first pitch shortly after 7:00pm.

The St. Louis Arch over center field provides a premiere skyline view.

Game 14: Busch Stadium, St. Louis, MO
July 25, 2012 – Dodgers 2, Cardinals 3

Category	Rank	Comments
Best Design	19	The brick-and-steel architecture is reminiscent of Union Station. I found it challenging to change levels though.
Best View	5	The St. Louis Arch is perfectly centered over center field. Great downtown view.
Best Hot Dog	26	The $4.25 "hot dog" is crap. I didn't find a signature dog at Busch Stadium. I'd elect for the Bratwurst next time though.
Best Mascot	10	*Fredbird* is a well-known red bird, active both at games and in the community.
Best Fans	6	Impressive when it's 102-degrees during the first pitch, and 37,841 Wednesday fans still show up.
Best-Looking Females	21	If you're in high school, then you're set. But the 20's and 30's crowd is lacking.
Best Entertainment	14	The kiss Cam and T-shirt launch is okay, but the Cardinals Girls' jumbotron photo shoot was... real nice.
Best Tradition	20	I'm a sucker for closer songs. Jason Motte enters to "Brain Stew" by *Green Day*.
Best Feature	25	The best feature is the view, perfectly aligned with the St. Louis Arch over center field.
Final Rank	17th	Modern style that fits St. Louis, without the unique "Wow!" factor that might boost it higher.

CHAPTER 18
Hotlanta

A few days before I arrive to Atlanta, I find a place to stay on Couchsurfing with two friends named Ted and David. On Saturday morning, I arrive to their house on the northern edge of Piedmont Park. I tentatively plan to go to the Braves game in the evening.

As I'm resting on their couch during the day, I check my latest Couchsurfing messages. I receive an unread offer from a thirty-three-year-old pharmaceutical scientist:

> *Hey Cody, I'm relatively new to hosting but you are welcome to stay in my high-rise condo in midtown Atlanta. I am a Braves fan but won't be going to the Braves game Saturday, but if you'd like I'd love to take you there Sunday. I have season tickets and my friend who was supposed to go with me is stuck in California for work so I have an extra ticket. —Steve*

I reply to Steve, telling him I already have a host, but am all-in for the Sunday game. He picks me up the next day, and I come outside carrying my Camelbak, sunscreen, and two jumbo bags of peanuts. It feels a little weird hopping into a car with a complete stranger, but as it turns out, Steve is a classic character. He's originally from Hong Kong, so we break the ice reminiscing about all the Asian countries we've both visited. His PhD from Pitt is in the exact same field as my ex-girlfriend's PhD at UCLA, so I actually know a little bit about his professional community. On top of that, he tells me about a recent research trip to the Amazon, where he slept in a hammock while floating downstream on a barge. *That's crazy Steve, because in early May, I did the exact same thing!*

When we get to the parking lot at Turner Field, Steve points out that we're driving on top of the former grounds of Atlanta-Fulton County Stadium. As we drive around the outer perimeter, I notice we're next to the original blue concrete wall that once ran along the outfield. Growing up, my Dad used to tell me stories about visiting this place when he was a kid. My Grandpa spent several years stationed at the Marine Corps base in Parris Island, South Carolina, and every summer, he would load up the Station Wagon and take my dad and his brothers on a baseball road trip to Atlanta. Now that I'm here, it almost feels like I'm walking in their shadow.

On July 14, 1968, on one of their road trips, my Dad witnessed "Hammerin'" Hank Aaron smack his 500th career home run at this exact location. Every fan at Atlanta Stadium that day was issued a card that read: *Possession of this card is proof I was there when Hank Aaron hit his 500th Home Run.* I know this because my Dad still has it, forty-four years later. My Dad's birthday was yesterday, and I think he's happy knowing I'm celebrating it in a place where he has such fond baseball memories.

Steve and I outside of the gates at Turner Field. His Tomahawk Chop
T-shirt is awesome.

Turner Field's Dixie Dog gave me a food orgasm. So good.

Game 15: Turner Field, Atlanta, GA
July 29, 2012 – Phillies 2, Braves 6

Category	Rank	Comments
Best Design	21	Before opening for the Braves in 1997, Turner Field served as the 1996 Summer Olympics Stadium.
Best View	22	The best view is from the Coca-Cola patio on the upper deck in left field.
Best Hot Dog	2	Dixie Dog: Foot-long fried dog with BBQ pulled pork, nacho cheese, southern coleslaw, and pickles.
Best Mascot	19	*Homer The Brave* is a double entendre, holding the most clever mascot nickname in the game.
Best Fans	10	Did you see them protest the "infield fly" in the 2012 Wild Card game? Bottles on bottles on bottles.
Best-Looking Females	6	Mm-mmm. I love Georgia Peaches.
Best Entertainment	11	@bravesorganist on Twitter connects fans with Braves organist Matthew Kaminski. Request a song.
Best Tradition	1	Nothing beats the Braves' Tomahawk Chant. Nothing.
Best Feature	19	Above left field, a giant Coca-Cola bottle shoots fireworks after each Braves home run.
Final Rank	8th	The Dixie Dog, Tomahawk Chant, and Georgia peaches could keep me preoccupied for an entire summer.

112

CHAPTER 19
Cincy Skyline

Opening Day in Cincinnati is a tradition alike nowhere else, where kids and adults indulge in a citywide holiday to celebrate the beginning of a new season. The Opening Day festivities include ice cream socials, eating contests, and Budweiser Clydesdales, all in addition to their hallmark event, The Findlay Market Parade.

In the early-1800's, the boomtown of Cincinnati established enough population and wealth along the Ohio River to become the largest inland city in the United States. It's considered to be the first "American" city because it wasn't developed as a byproduct of offshore immigration. This makes Cincinnati a fitting home for the Reds, the first professional baseball team in a sport credited as America's pastime. The pageantry of Opening Day in Cincinnati is a tribute to their longtime history, and for many years, the Reds' Opening Day starter traditionally threw out the first pitch of the regular season, before any of the other Major League games began.

When I arrive to the Cincinnati Greyhound Station on Tuesday, July 31st, I find the grey sedan I'm looking for. I walk across the parking lot and climb inside.

"You ready to sit next to the biggest asshole in Cincy

tonight?!" I excitedly ask Kenny, whom I haven't seen since our softball days in LA.

On Facebook a few days ago, Kenny randomly noticed that we'd both be passing through Cincinnati at the same time. Being that we're both huge baseball fans, we made plans for the Reds game tonight. Coincidentally, the Padres are in town from San Diego, and I'm ready to start a ruckus.

The first thing I do inside Great American Ballpark is scout out the hot dogs. I'm hungry, and being the committed journalist that I am, I want to judge before I start drinking. I notice a place called *Skyline Chili* with a 'Cheese Coney' for $4.75. It seems extremely popular, but the normal concession stands have a $5.50 item called the Big Red Smokey. I've purchased all of my dogs at traditional ballpark stands thus far, so I ignore *Skyline* and go for the Smokey.

Kenny and I find our seats and start getting rowdy with some guys behind us from the University of Cincinnati. There are also three drunk girls in front of us celebrating a twenty-first birthday. This leads to more chaos, and ultimately, our group debauchery gets displayed on the jumbotron late in the game. At the end of a fun night, though, the Padres lose a tight one, 7-6.

Two days later, on Thursday, I return to Great American Ballpark with my Couchsurfing host, Samantha. The scorching day game is the last of a four-game series between the Padres and Reds. Again, I bask in the heat with my Camelbak, sunscreen, and jumbo bag of peanuts.

Near the end of the game, I become aware of the most ridiculous ballpark promotion in the history of ballpark promotions. The Reds are up 9-4 with one out in the top of the ninth, getting ready to close the game. It's not a "save" situation for the pitcher, so I'm surprised by how rambunctious and loud the fans are, especially the kids. I've attended over a hundred Major League games in my life, and never has a home crowd acted like this with a five run lead. Then, with two strikes on the second batter of the inning, the ENTIRE crowd starts chanting, "PIZ-ZA! PIZ-ZA! PIZ-ZA!

"Umm, Samantha? What's going on? Why are...?" I begin, completely baffled. She proceeds to explain, offering enlightenment as to why the crowd is acting like a bunch of lunatics. Apparently, during the 2012 season, every time the Reds combine to throw eleven or more strikeouts in a game, ALL ticket holders win a free small pizza from La Rosa's Pizzeria, AND a free scoop of Homemade Brand Ice Cream from United Dairy Farmers. Fans are given seven days to redeem the prize.

As she finishes explaining, the Reds get their tenth strikeout. The crowd goes ballistic. Kids jump and flop down the stairways, and the adults bang on the seats like gorillas. Great American Ballpark has transformed into the great American jungle, with a bunch of freakish animals howling from the canopy. There are now two outs in the ninth inning, with one opportunity remaining to secure the eleventh strikeout.

The phenomenon intensifies. Before every pitch, the stadium echoes, "PIZ-ZA! PIZ-ZA! PIZ-ZA!" It's like a Gregorian chant, thundering towards the sky. Even though I'm laughing my face off, I start doing it too, like an idiot against my own team! "PIZ-ZA! PIZ-ZA! PIZ-ZA!" It reminds me of the climatic scene at the end of the movie *Rudy*, except this is real life, and we're not witnessing anything remotely spectacular. We're just screaming for pizza like a kindergarten field trip gone wrong. After issuing a walk, the Reds pitcher throws two strikes against the Padres batter. It's now louder and more hectic than ever. "PIZ-ZA! PIZ-ZA! PIZ-ZA!"

With every fan dialed in, the next pitch is delivered. The Padres batter swings at it, but pops it up to the shortstop, ending the game in disappointing fashion in front of 22,396 afternoon fans. While the Reds players congratulate each other on a remarkable thirteenth win in fourteen games, a new echo reverberates through the crowd.

"Booooooooooooooo!! Booooooooooooooo!!" Kids cry and psychotically scream at their parents, "I! WANT! PIZ-ZAAA!!!!!" *What a brilliant marketing ploy.*

As Samantha and I exit the jungle after the game, we pass *Skyline Chili* in the concourse.

"How'd you rank the Cheese Coney the other night?" she pokes.

"I didn't get it. I had the Big Red Smokey," I guiltily admit.

"What?!" she reacts, "You can't come here and not eat the Cheese Coney! That's THE hot dog in Cincinnati – It's our staple!"

Gulp.

"Don't worry," she remarks, "I'll take you to the old Skyline up on the hill. The food's the exact same, and it's way cheaper."

Nicholas Lambrinides founded *Skyline Chili* thirty-seven years after immigrating to the United States from Kastoria, Greece. Mr. Lambrinides brought his family recipes from overseas, and spent years in America crafting his chili to perfection. In 1949, Nicholas and his three sons opened their first diner at the top of Price Hill in Cincinnati, naming it *Skyline* to reflect the restaurant's beautiful downtown view. Years later, after Nicholas passed away, his son William noted,

"Dad always said, 'Don't change a thing with the recipe – don't add anything, don't take out anything, it's perfect the way it is'."

As Samantha watches me chow down my first Cheese Coney near the University of Cincinnati campus, every part of me wishes I could give a hug to Mr. Nicholas Lambrinides. It's incredible. Taken directly from their website, this is their modest description:

> *Skyline's classic Cheese Coney is a specialty-made hot dog in a steamed bun, with mustard, covered with our secret-recipe chili, diced onions, and shredded cheddar cheese.*

"Rumor has it they put chocolate and cinnamon in it," Samantha mentions. I extract those flavors as I chew, and continue eating and eating and eating. When I'm finished, I tackle the chili-cheese fries, and then the signature 3-way: spaghetti topped with chili topped with shredded cheddar cheese.

Back home, I'm actually a bit of a nutrition freak, but don't get me wrong; I *love* to eat. A couple of years ago, I ate a ten-by-ten cheeseburger (ten patties) at In-'N-Out Burger in California, and successfully completed the Giant Burger eating challenge in Laughlin, Nevada. I even ate twenty-one pancakes at an IHOP one time, in attempt to break the restaurant record, but fell short. Sometimes I wonder if I'm a long lost relative of Adam Richman, the host of Travel Channel's *Man vs. Food*.

On an off-topic note, if anyone from the Travel Channel does happen to read this, or any other TV executive for that matter, I'd like to formally nominate myself for a new show: *Man vs. Booze*. As host, I would travel the country slammin' down mythical drinks of beastly proportions, with an obstacle course to complete at the end of each episode.

Though I don't remember the exact cost, the orgasm-in-my-mouth Cheese Coney from was under two dollars. *Two Dollars!* As Samantha and I get ready to leave, I notice several pictures hanging on the wall. They're photos of various celebrities eating at this particular Skyline Chili, which is now their flagship location. I see President Barack Obama, pop-singer Nick Lachey, and talk show host Jerry Springer.

"Obama came here on his campaign tour," Samantha mentions, "And Nick Lachey is from Cincinnati."

"What about Jerry Springer?" I inquire, "That's random."

"Oh, people love him here," she tells me, "Before he was famous, he was our Mayor."

Kenny (left), me (center), and his friend (whose name I also don't remember) in front of Great American Ballpark. Check out the people behind us – Who brings an oxygen tank to a baseball game?

The Ohio River sits directly behind Great American Ballpark.

Game 16: Great American Ballpark, Cincinnati, OH
July 31, 2012 – Padres 6, Reds 7
August 2, 2012 – Padres 4, Reds 9

Category	Rank	Comments
Best Design	6	Sits on the Ohio river, in downtown, with a steamboat above center field. There isn't a bad seat in the house.
Best View	3	Sit high for a great view of the Ohio River. One of the few ballparks in baseball with a waterfront location.
Best Hot Dog	3	The $4.75 Cheese Coney from Skyline Chili will take your taste buds on a ride.
Best Mascot	25	Three mascots are two too many! Gapper, Rosie Red, and Mr. Redlegs overwhelm adults, let alone kids.
Best Fans	15	For a first place team, attendance and crowd noise seem meager at best.
Best-Looking Females	18	The Cincinnati and Xavier campuses are nearby, and the ladies flock to support center fielder Drew Stubbs. "Marry Me, Drew?" signs galore.
Best Entertainment	21	The sponsored "Smile Cam" was original, but the sound system is too quiet.
Best Tradition	4	Opening Day! The city holiday is an annual tradition featuring the Findlay Market Parade.
Best Feature	2	The built-in steamboat above center field shoots out fire after each Reds strikeout.
Final Rank	3rd	Great coney, great view, great tradition – Cincinnati is just a stellar destination for baseball.

CHAPTER 20
Lions And Tigers (Hate Da Bears)

I was a Geography major in college, so I'd like to start off this chapter with a nerdy trivia question: If you draw a straight line on a map due south from downtown Detroit, what is the first country you would hit (besides the United States)?

An hour before I arrive to Detroit, my bus passes through Toledo, Ohio. It was near here, in the town of Defiance, where a historic baseball card collection was discovered back in February. A family was cleaning out the house of Carl Hench, who had left the estate to his daughter when he died in the 1940's. In October 2011, his daughter passed away, leaving her will to twenty nieces and nephews. The cousins began sorting through the house and came across their grandfather's century-old collection of approximately 700 baseball cards in the attic. Included were well-preserved gems featuring Hall of Famers Honus Wagner, Cy Young, and Detroit Tigers legend Ty Cobb.

Last night, at the National Sports Collectors Convention in Baltimore, thirty-seven of the cards were auctioned through a live and online bidding process. The combined sale brought revenue of $566,132, which will be split between all twenty cousins. One Honus Wagner card fetched $239,000 after it was judged to be in perfect condition by Professional Sports Authenticator. Heritage Auctions will sell the remainder of the cards, many of which are in pristine condition, over the next several years. Those are estimated to net an additional three million dollars for the family.

I arrive to Detroit early on this Friday afternoon, giving me hours of free time before the seven-o'clock game at Comerica Park. The Greyhound station is located between Bricktown and Corktown in an old, rundown neighborhood on the outer southwest banks of downtown. Most people in my position would likely hail a taxi, go east on Howard Street, pass under the bridge, and get dropped off in the nicer, more populated area of the city. I do the exact opposite. I go west on Howard Avenue, by foot.

I soon pass an ancient, spray-painted Cadillac Seville with a shattered back window. It looks like it has been sitting there for ten years, and the overall scene doesn't give me a warm, fuzzy feeling. With every questionable character that I pass, my pace quickens. There aren't any aluminum trash bins on fire, but it wouldn't be a surprising sight here in the wintertime. I walk three more blocks, and make a right at Trumbull Street.

As I move north, my nerves begin to calm. The neighborhood becomes a tad friendlier as I adjust to my environment. Fortunately, I know exactly where I'm going, and exactly how I'm going to spend my afternoon. It's so close to the bus station, I'd be a fool to skip it.

I finally reach the intersection I've been looking for. It's Michigan Avenue and Trumbull, infamously known as "The Corner". In Detroit, this land is sacred. It's a place where fathers built relationships with their sons, where a city of blue-collar workers found identity, where love was harnessed and tales were told, where records were set and championships won. "The Corner" is the nickname and location of the historic Tiger Stadium.

I quickly cross the street and walk west along Michigan Avenue. Along the north edge of the sidewalk is the original wrought-iron entrance gates. I find an opening and walk inside.

Standing before me is a huge lot of empty land where the stadium once stood. In the middle of the field, though, rests the weathered remains of a baseball diamond. The ground is uneven, the field not manicured, the bases gone, but it's a diamond of legacy. I trudge across the vacant field of untreated grass until I reach the batter's box. It's here where Babe Ruth smashed the longest verifiable home run in the history of baseball, a shot to dead center field in 1921 that flew out of the stadium and landed near the intersection behind the ballpark. His mammoth blast is reported to have traveled between 575 and 600 feet on the fly.

Other than the field itself, nearly every other aspect of Tiger Stadium has been fully demolished. Besides the gate along Michigan Avenue, the only remaining feature is the iconic 125-foot flagpole, which stood just left of dead center field in front of the fence.

I set my backpack down to walk the perimeter of the field. This was the place where Lou Gehrig voluntarily took a day off after playing 2,130 consecutive games, a staggering record that was considered unbreakable until Cal Ripken Jr. broke it fifty-six years later. Due to Gehrig's terminal condition of what is now known as Lou Gehrig's Disease (ALS), he never played in another game again.

When I reach the outfield, I jog along the fence line to

get an idea of the dimensions. I can tell where the wall used to stand, because the grass distinctively grows different in the field of play. I touch the flagpole, and stand where the fence once stood in dead center field, a whopping 440 feet from home plate. As I come back around to the infield, I realize I've never run the bases at a past or present Major League field. *Since I'm here, why not?* I'm particularly fascinated because Tiger Stadium opened on April 20, 1912, the same day as Fenway Park. The greatest legends of the game played on this infield, and it's one of the oldest baseball diamonds that still exists.

I decide that if I'm going to be a nerd and actually run the bases, then I'm going to be a super nerd and run them as fast as I can. I take my stance in the batter's box, weight back, and imagine a Major League fastball. I cradle my invisible bat and take a quick swing, driving my hips through the ball. I watch it sail towards the gap as I start running, dropping my bat near the plate. As I round first base, I pump my arms as hard as I can, gaining full steam ahead. I fly through second with a triple in mind, but the third base coach is waving me around! The ball must've caromed deep in the trenches of center field – I can make it all the way home! My legs scurry quicker than ever as I come around the horn, my face clenched with determination. Home plate is less than ninety feet away, and the crowd cheers wildly as I run like the wind. Just before I cross home plate, a smile beams across my face. I score standing up, an inside-the-park home run! When my left foot taps down on home plate, I think about Detroit's four World Series championship teams that played here, including the 1984 squad that beat the Padres in five games.

Another thought crosses my mind as I snap back to reality. At the intersection right now, on "The Corner", there's probably a couple guys sitting in a beat up Cadillac, hunched over in hysterical laughter, mocking and pointing at my white ass laboring around the bases. They can't contain themselves, and are gasping, "Tell me he's not doing it. Yuuup, he's doin' it! White boy be sprintin' the bases at Tiger Stadium!"

Lastly, if you draw a line due south from downtown Detroit, the first country you'll hit is Canada. Trick question.

This is what remains of the original Tiger Stadium at "The Corner". The 125-foot flagpole (shown top-left) stood in play on the near side of the center field fence, which was 440 feet from home plate.

Game 17: Comerica Park, Detroit, MI
August 3, 2012 – Indians 2, Tigers 10

Category	Rank	Comments
Best Design	3	The roof, flagpole, and big wooden seats behind home plate blend the old with the new.
Best View	4	Comerica Park faces south towards Canada, with a perfect view of the GM Towers and the rest of downtown Detroit.
Best Hot Dog	21	No team dog. I went for the $4.25 Ballpark Frank, but next time would do the Kosher.
Best Mascot	15	No surprise – the mascot is an orange Tiger named *Paws* who likes to dance.
Best Fans	8	The Tigers make up Detroit's DNA as much as the auto industry. 41,502 Friday night fans.
Best-Looking Females	9	Good news, gentleman! There are good-looking women in all age brackets.
Best Entertainment	20	The Chevrolet Fountain shoots water while a tiger growl is broadcasted after each home run.
Best Tradition	7	Journey's *Don't Stop Believin'*, a song set in Detroit, plays in the middle of the eighth inning.
Best Feature	12	The eyes of two giant tigers above the scoreboard light up in red after each home run and win.
Final Rank	4th	Of the modern built ballparks, Comerica has an incredibly unique blend of old style and new comfort.

CHAPTER 21
Cleveland Rocks!

On Saturday morning, August the fourth, I receive the following message on Couchsurfing:

> Hey Cody! Your trip sounds totally awesome! You are welcome to crash on my couch. I wish I could make it to the game with you… but I play a softball double header at 8:30 and 9:30 on Monday night. Regardless, your trip sounds really interesting, so you are welcome to crash if you want. I work Monday from 8–4:30 and wouldn't be able to show you around a ton, but we could grab dinner or a drink before the game! Cheers, Lauren

After visiting my aunt in Akron for the weekend, I arrive to Cleveland at 4:30 on Monday afternoon. The bus station is just a few blocks from Lauren's office, and she swings by to pick me up before heading to the ballpark.

My Couchsurfing hosts have been great thus far, but none of them are quite like Lauren. She's good-looking, is a sweetheart, and most importantly, a huge baseball fan. She's also certified to sail a boat anywhere around the world. When Lauren responded to my couch search in Cleveland, I honestly didn't know how to reply. Disguised in her message was a memo that screamed, "I'm awesome!" In life, every once in a while, you will come across someone who exudes particular qualities and characteristics that you find special. They're the people who, one minute after meeting, make you feel like you've known them forever. That's the case with Lauren. We just "get" each other, and the fact that she's a fun-loving Indians girl makes it even better. It's a beautiful afternoon in Cleveland, and there's something in the air that foreshadows a memorable evening ahead.

As we look for street parking near the ballpark, Lauren blurts, "Oh, I forgot to tell you! I have free tickets for us tonight, so I'm going to come with you until I have to go to softball."

"Really? That's awesome! How'd you get 'em?"

"I volunteer for an organization that gives me two ticket vouchers for every eight hours. Tonight's one of the eligible games, but they're only for the upper deck or the bleachers. Is that alright?"

"Are you kidding? Free?" I chuckle. "*Love* it."

"Ugh, I hate parallel parking," she interjects as we pull next to an empty space. "And this is a brand new car."

"I'm actually a great parallel parker if you want me..."

Before I can finish my offer, Lauren has shot out of the driver's side door. Her car is now parked in the middle of the street, so I can only assume we're playing an unspoken game of Chinese fire drill. Crazy girl. As I get behind the wheel, put the car in reverse, and look back, she makes it nearly impossible to focus. Apparently the passenger seat is her personal dressing room, because I see heels and everything else flailing across my line of sight as I look out the back window. No joke, in thirty seconds, Lauren has turned into a human transformer. She throws on all of her softball attire over her work clothes, and then removes her blouse from underneath her T-shirt, all before I could turn off the car. I couldn't even believe it. What an odd talent.

After a couple of beers at Thirsty Parrot, we cross the street and enter Progressive Field thirty minutes before game time. Per my usual routine, we take a lap around the lower concourse as Lauren tells me about the stadium. When we get to right field, we walk down the staircase above the outfield wall. Lauren receives a phone call, and I'm not paying any attention whatsoever to her conversation. Then she hangs up.

"I didn't tell you earlier because I didn't want to get your hopes up," she reveals, "but I have a friend who works in the front office for the Indians. He wants to come meet you."

Less than three minutes later, Lauren and I are with her friend in an elevator shaft, embarking on a behind-the-scenes tour of Progressive Field. When the doors open, I feel like I'm in a movie. We're standing in the underground tunnel below the stadium, a place I've never been to in any ballpark.

Family members of the players occupy the first couple rooms that we pass in the long tunnel. Then we go by the X-ray room, the medical room, the weight room, the media conference room, the batting cages, and finally the doors to the clubhouse.

"We can't go in there right now," we're told, "but let's keep walking." Soon we reach an underground parking area at the northwest end of the stadium. "This is the players lot," our guide explains. He points out a large, industrious garage door on the far side. "That actually goes to Quicken Loans Arena. When the Cavs were good during the LeBron era, Tom Brady, Giselle and other celebrities would actually park here on our side and get transported underneath the street. The underground tunnel is set up for the Cavs and Indians to help each other out."

He briefly shows Lauren and I the executive offices, and then we retreat back to the curved section on the tunnel, presumably behind home plate. "There's one more place I'd like to show you," he tells us. We suddenly turn down a sloped hallway labeled "Dugout Suites."

As we approach the bottom of the hallway, our guide greets an usher and flashes his front office badge. "We'll be in suite five," he informs the woman. We turn and walk down another curved hallway, getting closer to the field.

When we reach the fifth door, we enter an incredible room that could easily be mistaken for a corporate lunch lounge – huge private bathroom, full kitchen, leather couches, multiple flatscreen TV's. We walk through the room, out another door, and climb a small staircase. I look out and can't believe my eyes... *Am I dreaming?*

We are now standing directly behind home plate. Acting as a transparent backstop, only a metal screen separates us from the field of play. It curves around the bottom of the diamond from one dugout to the other, and houses ten individual Dugout Suites. I can nearly touch the field with my fingertips as we watch the first inning from the same point-of-view as the catcher and the umpire.

"Hey Cody, look up to your right," he prods. I turn to find the live game playing on the TV above us. I see only five people in the picture frame: the pitcher, the catcher, the batter, the umpire, and me! *Okay, I am definitely dreaming.* "You can do whatever you want, just don't wave or make gestures at the camera," he tells me.

I immediately call my brother back home in San Diego, who has access to the MLB-TV Internet package.

"Hey, are you home right now? ...Yeah? Flip on the Indians game." I wait a minute, and then I ask, "Do you recognize anyone in the picture?" My brother's reaction is extraordinary. "I'll tell you about it later," I reply, "But hey, take a picture for me. I gotta go."

I turn back to Lauren's friend to ask him a question. "Out of curiosity, how much does a suite like this go for?"

"It's usually a corporate package deal," he says. "When the ballpark first opened and attendance was high, this was known as Million Dollar Row. It was $100,000 per season with a 10-year commitment."

Lauren is soaking up the moment just as much as I am. We've somehow parlayed *free* ticket vouchers into the most *expensive* seats in the house.

As the bottom of the first inning comes to a close, our guide tells us he needs to get back to work. As we all stand up to leave, he pulls two tickets from his pocket and hands them to us.

"I printed these in my office," he says. "The suite is yours for the rest of the night."

The next morning, I wake up early on Lauren's couch. The DVD menu for the movie *Major League*, featuring Charlie Sheen as "Wild Thing" Ricky Vaughn, is still streaming on the TV in front of me. After a quick breakfast, Lauren drives me to the Greyhound station on her way to work. After an unbelievable night in Cleveland, the time has already come to leave for Pittsburgh.

Me (far left) making my ESPN debut from inside the Dugout Suite.

Lauren and I feeling ecstatic about our new seats behind home plate.

Game 18: Progressive Field, Cleveland, OH
August 6, 2012 – Twins 14, Indians 3

Category	Rank	Comments
Best Design	20	"Mini" Green Monster in left field. Try and count all 115 luxury boxes (Hint: there are ten behind home plate)
Best View	14	Nice skyline view in the heart of downtown Cleveland.
Best Hot Dog	20	The $5.00 Mega Dog with Bertman Ballpark Mustard is subpar.
Best Mascot	18	Fuzzy, pink creature *Slider* is in the Mascot HOF and on Twitter @SliderTheMascot.
Best Fans	23	Fans gave a standing ovation to the relief pitcher after Cleveland allowed 10 runs in the second inning. The 90's era of 455 consecutive sellouts is long gone.
Best-Looking Females	17	When you're already with a girl, it's difficult to scout the rest. This general score is accurate and fair though.
Best Entertainment	16	Hot dog races, dancing condiments, and big screen games help distract the fans from reality.
Best Tradition	16	*Wild Thing?* My heart sings to the Indian drum in the outfield bleachers – Groovy!
Best Feature	27	Nineteen vertical toothbrush-style light towers and a corkscrew-shaped wind turbine on the roof.
Final Rank	24th	The rankings lie. This is a beautiful venue set in a perfect cityscape.

133

CHAPTER 22
Black & Yellow, Black & Yellow

Pittsburgh was one of the few cities that I figured out long before I embarked from home. After I announced the ballpark trip to my family, my Mom mentioned it to one of the regional sales reps at her company. Bill lives in Pittsburgh, and before I could blink, he and I were exchanging emails, talking on the phone, and finalizing my itinerary.

A month ago, while I was in Oregon, I confirmed to Bill that I would be arriving on the seventh of August and leaving the next day. Shortly thereafter, I received an e-mail confirmation from the Wyndham Grand Pittsburgh, an upscale hotel located directly across the river from PNC Park. Bill had purchased a room for me using his credit cards points, an incredibly generous act from someone I had yet to meet.

While I was in Chicago a few weeks later, Bill called to tell me about the field level tickets he had secured for my visit. He also asked if I'd be interested in a tour of PNC Park on the morning of the game. When I expressed my interest at the time, I had no idea it'd be my second ballpark tour in eighteen hours.

When I arrive to Pittsburgh after my two-hour bus ride from Cleveland, I walk ten blocks through downtown to my hotel. As I enter my room, I take in the panoramic view of Point State Park and Heinz Field across the Allegheny River. After becoming a battle-tested road warrior over the past several weeks, I'm still not sure what I've done to deserve the Dugout Suite in Cleveland and the Wyndham Grand in Pittsburgh. After dropping my bag and watching a few minutes of SportsCenter, I go downstairs, walk along the river, cross the 6th Street Bridge, and find Bill and his son Luke standing outside of PNC Park.

It's the perfect summer day in Pittsburgh – warm, sunny, clear skies – which makes the tour of PNC Park that much more spectacular. Our guide takes us all over the ballpark, showing us the press boxes, The Lexus Club, the Suites Level, and the Trib Total Media Hall of Fame Club. Then, for my second time in less than a day, we go underneath the seats into the player's tunnel.

As Bill, Luke and I follow our tour guide, he shows us the same doors I've recently become familiar with: the medical room, the X-ray room, the weight room, the media room, and the manager's office. Suddenly, we stop next to the Umpire's Lounge. Our tour guide points out that every other sign in the tunnel has Braille markings under the text. Humorously, though, the Umpire's Lounge does not.

Inside the batting cage, there's a list on the wall of every batting champion in the history of the franchise. Incredibly, the Pirates have produced twenty-five National League batting champions since 1900, which is more than any other team in Major League Baseball history. Nearly half of those batting titles belong to Honus Wagner and Roberto Clemente, who won eight times and four times, respectively.

While I'm on the topic of Roberto Clemente, I'd like to pay my substantial respect to him by sharing his story for my casual readers. From 1955–1972, Roberto Clemente played right field for the Pittsburgh Pirates. On December 31, 1972, three months after recording his 3,000th career hit on his final at-bat of the season, Clemente died in a fatal plane crash near his home island of Puerto Rico. He was en route delivering supplies to earthquake victims in Nicaragua, a symbolic act that embodied his well-known philanthropic nature. Today, more so than his decorated accomplishments on the field, Clemente is remembered for his commitment to humanitarian work off of it. Major League Baseball honors him by annually presenting the Roberto Clemente Award to the current player who best exemplifies charitable qualities throughout the season. Clemente finished his career as a 15-time All-Star, 12-time Gold Glove Award winner, 4-time National League batting champion, and 2-time World Series winner. He also won the 1966 National League MVP, and became the 1971 World Series MVP the year before his death. In 1973, the Baseball Writers Association of America voted to waive Clemente's five-year grace period for the Hall of Fame. The exclusive voting decision marks the only time an exemption has ever occurred in Hall of Fame history, which allowed Clemente to be enshrined into Cooperstown just months after his passing.

As I sit with Bill and his family during the third inning later that night, I notice a hot dog vendor desperately trying to sell his culinary goods as he labors up and down the stairs. But, with the Pirates deep in the playoff hunt, the fans are intently focused on the game.

"Hot dogs! Hot dogs! Who wants a hot dog?" he bellows across the quiet crowd on the first base side. His appearance is best described as a rough, slightly overweight, middle-aged man, fitting the Pittsburgh stereotype you'd expect to find at a Steelers game.

"Three dollar hot dogs here! Who wants a hot dog?" he continues. The strap around his neck is heavy as he pesters our section. The Diamondbacks are batting, so his voice booms across the tame audience.

"C'mon, hot dogs here!" he persists.

Still, though, no one calls out to him. As the Pirates record their final out of the inning, he walks back up the staircase and dejectedly moves on.

During the middle of the third inning, Pittsburgh's mascot, Pirate Parrot, storms onto the field with a hotdog launcher. It's essentially a pressurized air gun that propels flying franks into the crowd. People go bonkers for this, especially when they realize it has enough firepower to reach the upper deck. Fans rise to their feet, wave their arms, and scream crazy things that they think will help. The fiasco doesn't last long, however, and ends when the bottom half of the inning is ready to begin. As everyone returns to their seat, the ballpark noise drops back to its normal volume.

Immediately following the ensuing pitch, I hear familiar footsteps marching down the stairs. I know who it is before I see him, as even a deaf person would recognize this heavy stomp. It's our rough, slightly overweight, middle-aged hot dog vendor. He's returned again, this time with a brand new sales pitch.

"HEY!" he shouts, "SO WHO WANTS MY HOT DOG NOW??!!"

Our section bursts into laughter, and his hot dog sales spike by the dozen.

Luke and I on the field during our tour at PNC Park.

Me keeping the benches warm in the Pirates dugout.

Game 19: PNC Park, Pittsburgh, PA
August 7, 2012 – Diamondbacks 10, Pirates 4

Category	Rank	Comments
Best Design	1	Classic style, riverfront setting, and limestone exterior make PNC the best downtown ballpark in baseball.
Best View	2	Hangs on the Allegheny River, overlooking three steel bridges linking to the heart of downtown Pittsburgh.
Best Hot Dog	22	The $3.00 "hot dog" tasted better than pricier options elsewhere, but don't miss out on a sandwich from Primanti Brothers.
Best Mascot	2	*Pirate Parrot* is truly a sidekick for the Bucs. He loves to prank and mock the opposing players before the game.
Best Fans	9	When the Steelers and Penguins are out of season, the Pirates get all the attention.
Best-Looking Females	14	Similar to Detroit, there's fun for all ages!
Best Entertainment	10	Good scoreboard guessing games. I found the CD-player giveaway hilariously outdated.
Best Tradition	27	Pittsburgh is the city of black and yellow. All of its professional teams wear the same colors, which are the colors of the city.
Best Feature	21	Statues of Hall of Famers Honus Wagner, Willie Stargell, Bill Mazeroski, and Roberto Clemente (right field wall is also 21-feet tall in honor of #21 Roberto Clemente)
Final Rank	7th	Many believe PNC is one of the best venues in baseball, and that's fully reflected in the first two categories.

CHAPTER 23
City of Brotherly Love

When I was working in LA, I had the opportunity to visit my company's corporate headquarters in New York City. To this day, I remember my first visit inside the office of our Chief Operating Officer. He was reclined in his chair, one foot propped on the desk, tennis ball in one hand, and a two-liter of Diet Coke in the other. A massive chalkboard hung on the wall behind him, displaying an orange Nike swoosh sticker in the top-right corner. The rest of the slate was wiped clean, except for six bold words written across the middle: *FAIL TO PLAN. PLAN TO FAIL.*

My ex-COO's formula consciously ticks through my head as I arrive to Philadelphia *without a plan*; not a clue as to what I'm doing or where I need to go. I know I'm staying with my Dad's cousin across the river, but she works late tonight, and the Phillies game starts in an hour. Reminiscent of my situation in St. Louis, I am desperate for a place to store my travel bag before I go to the ballpark. Basically, I need to do three things: Figure. It. Out.

The Philadelphia Greyhound Station is an absolute nightmare when I get off the bus. It reminds me of Bangkok's train depot during Songkran, the Thai New Year celebrated in

April. Crowded masses shuffle in confusion like Charlie Sheen on a Sunday morning. And the only employee I can find would be better off eating a Snickers bar in the break room. After spending twenty critical minutes trying to inquire about bag storage, I give up any hope for help. Disgruntled, I exit the building and turn right.

As I mope west down Filbert Street, my body feels fatigued, my spirit depleted. I've spent the day listening to the wheels on the bus go 'round and 'round all the way across Pennsylvania, while my grumpy driver repeatedly screamed at passengers. Today's saga has distorted my outlook, and to be honest, I don't feel excited to be in Philadelphia. What I want, what I really need, is a friend – someone to restore my positivity.

Even though I'm in a different state of mind than I was in St. Louis, I realize I have no choice but to locate a hotel. After a few blocks, I find one near City Hall, and walk inside with the hope that somebody will help me.

The interior of the Philadelphia Marriott Downtown is extravagant. The grand lobby is comprised of restaurants, concierge desks, chandeliers, and the Circ Lounge, which is bustling with patrons. I ignore the overwhelming environment and focus my senses on the task at hand. After crossing the lower level, I target a friendly-looking gentleman near the north entrance. He stands at a podium next to a sign: *Bellhop Desk*.

"How ya doin' sir?" I ask as I approach. "I'm actually not a guest here, but I do have a favor to ask… I'm on a trip to all the Major League ballparks, and I just got to town on the bus. I need to store my bag for a few hours while I'm at the Phillies game this evening. Is there any way you could help me out?"

The man gazes around the lobby like a seasoned

veteran, and then looks back at me. "I'll take it for you, but if anyone asks, I don't know a thing."

A sigh of relief exhales from my shoulders as I thank him graciously. While he's storing my bag in the back room, I open my wallet and realize I'm only carrying three dollars. When he returns, I tip him all the money I have as he hands me the bag tag.

"I actually have another question," I inquire, "I'm planning to ride SEPTA to Citizens Bank Park. What's the fastest way to get there?"

He starts to explain, then stops. "You know what? Follow me," he instructs. And before I know it, we're stampeding through the lobby towards the west end of the building.

As we walk, Bryan and I make conversation about our lives. I give him a quick synopsis of my summer, and he tells me about his twenty-three years working for Marriott. I casually mention that I'm twenty-five, and we laugh that he's been helping guests like me for almost as long as I've been alive.

We exit to the sidewalk and walk one block south. At the corner of the intersection, we get inside an elevator that drops us below the street. When we hit the bottom, the doors open to the sight of underground train tracks. We turn right and walk westbound.

Bryan is a short, stocky, African-American man who moves as quickly as I do. I would venture to guess he probably played linebacker in high school. More important than his appearance, however, is his moral character. He exudes qualities of a polite, professional, blue-collar citizen who works hard for his family. As he tells me about his wife, his kids, and his dreams for retirement, it's transparent that Bryan's priorities rest in family and faith. He's also steadfast in his commitment to customer service, helping me off the street like a VIP guest. I can't believe he's walking me all the way to the train stop!

When we finally reach the boarding platform, Bryan shows me how to purchase a fare to Citizens Bank Park. It's $1.55 per token, costing $3.10 for the roundtrip. I pull out my credit card, ready to swipe it through the machine.

"Ah man," he informs me, "It's cash only."

My stone cold stare says it all. I open my wallet to put my card away. "I need to run to the bank," I muster aloud, head sunken with disappointment.

"No, no, I'll cover you," he immediately insists.

Without giving me the opportunity to politely decline, Bryan pulls my three-dollar tip from his pocket and feeds the machine. Ten cents short, he uses a dollar bill of his own before collecting the ninety cents in change that spits back out.

I stand there speechless, my eyes glimmering with gratitude. As Bryan hands me two SEPTA tokens, my soul's faith in humanity reaches an all-time pinnacle. Of all the special moments on my trip, none have touched me as deeply as this random act of kindness. As I begin thanking him, he cuts me off.

"Don't worry about it," he responds with a smile, "I've been doing this long enough to know it'll come back to me. This is the City of Brotherly Love. Go enjoy the game."

As my train click-clacks down the tracks, I stare at Bryan out the window, filled with the grace of his generosity. The underlying message in my story is to inspire others to live their dream, but the spiritual quest of my own journey is to uncover the innate kindness of the human race. For me, Bryan's deed is a defining moment.

I arrive to Citizen's Bank Park barely in time for the

start of the game. As I reflect on what has just happened, I open my iPhone notes and type six bold words: *FAIL TO PLAN. MAKE A FRIEND.*

If any of my readers make it to downtown Philadelphia anytime soon, please do me a favor: Stop by the Marriott, show Bryan this chapter, and return the brotherly love that he so much deserves.

I arrived to Citizens Bank Park just in time for the start of the game.

Game 20: Citizens Bank Park, Philadelphia, PA
August 8, 2012 – Braves 12, Phillies 6

Category	Rank	Comments
Best Design	18	The left and right field fences are the most hitter-friendly dimensions in baseball.
Best View	21	CBP is built in South Philly with a hazy downtown view in the distance.
Best Hot Dog	9	Pay a little extra for the $5.50 Hatfield Grilled Hot Dog. Skip 9th St. Market concessions.
Best Mascot	4	The *Philly Phanatic* is epic – launches hot dogs into the crowd from his golf cart.
Best Fans	3	41,501 Wednesday night fans proves Philly has some of the best attendance numbers in MLB – CBP looked like the Red Sea.
Best-Looking Females	26	There's a saying, "You are what you eat," and some of these people look like cheesesteaks.
Best Entertainment	1	The "Move It Like Bernie" dance-off and the Jersey Shore-like "Flex Cam" are the two funniest segments in baseball.
Best Tradition	25	The *Rocky* theme song pumps up the crowd.
Best Feature	18	The cracked Liberty Bell hanging above center field lights up with stars after each Phillies home run.
Final Rank	15th	The fanfare and entertainment at CBP is electrifying, and the Philly Phanatic fits right in. Odd location though.

CHAPTER 24
The Land of Pleasant Living

Riding in the passenger seat of Colin's car, I bite through a Twizzler as we make the seventy-five-mile drive from Lancaster[10], Pennsylvania to Baltimore, Maryland. As I smack the red plastic in my mouth, I tell him about an unsettled rift that divides my family.

"My brother and I have an ongoing argument with my sister-in-law, who is from Connecticut," I explain. "She *loves* Twizzlers and hates Red Vines. We couldn't disagree more. Red Vines are superior."

"Are you kidding me?!" Colin protests. "Red Vines are terrible! How could you not like Twizzlers?!"

"This crap?" I mock, slapping the package. "Tastes like rubber! What is it with you people? Every East Coaster I know *loves* Twizzlers. But I GUAR-AN-TEE… if you ask anyone on the West Coast, they'll pick Red Vines."

"Seriously, Cody? You're telling me that the fundamental difference in our country is that West Coast

---

[10] Twizzlers are manufactured in Lancaster, Pennsylvania by Y&S Candies, Inc., a subsidiary of The Hershey Company. The American Licorice Company based in Union City, California owns Red Vines, their mainstream competitor.

people like Red Vines, and East Coasters like Twizzlers?"

"Yep, that's exactly what I'm saying."

Until yesterday, it had been three weeks since I'd last seen Colin in Milwaukee. After he and Emily finished their trip, Colin invited me to visit his hometown a couple hours outside of Philadelphia. Today, we're driving to watch the Orioles play at Camden Yards for my twenty-first, and his thirty-first, stop of the year.

Camden Yards is aptly named because it was formerly a freight yard at the street corners of Camden and Eutaw. Behind the park in right field is the B&O Warehouse, built by the *Baltimore & Ohio Railroad* at the turn of the Twentieth Century. The only player to ever hit the warehouse on the fly was Ken Griffey Jr., who did it during the Home Run Derby at the 1993 All-Star Game.

A few blocks east of Camden Yards is the historic seaport of Inner Harbor. This landmark tourist destination was once the childhood stomping grounds of George Herman Ruth, who was later nicknamed "The Babe." Babe Ruth was born two blocks northwest of Camden Yards at 216 Emory Street, and had a rough youth growing up around his father's saloon business in the neighborhood. Today, his childhood roots are commemorated in the *Babe's Dream* statue at the corner at Camden and Eutaw outside center field.

Further east along the harbor are the cobblestone streets of Fell's Point, the most popular entertainment and nightlife destination in the city. It's here, on Thames Street near the waterfront, where Colin takes me inside one of the most historic saloons in the country.

The Horse You Came In On was established in 1775, making it the oldest continually operated saloon in North America. It's rumored to be one of the most haunted destinations in Maryland, where it's the only saloon to operate before, during, and after the Prohibition era. Home to the original *Old No.7 Club*, the saloon sells more Jack Daniel's than any other bar in the state. Great American author Edgar Allan Poe, who wrote the poem *The Raven*[11], was last seen at *The Horse You Came In On* before his mysterious death in 1849.

The wood and brick interior of the saloon serves a clue to its history. With the authenticity of Disney's *Frontierland*, wagon wheels hang from the ceiling in the form of chandeliers, illuminating an otherwise dark establishment. Above the whiskey bar hangs an inspiring sign that speaks to my personality. It reads:

> *Life should not be a journey to the grave with the intention of arriving safely in a pretty and well preserved body, but rather to skid in broadside, thoroughly used up, totally worn out, and loudly proclaiming, "WOW, WHAT A RIDE!"*

I waste no time ordering a round of National Bohemian, or Natty Boh, the signature beer in the mid-Atlantic region. First brewed in 1885 in Baltimore, this legendary beer has become synonymous with the community, adopting the slogan "From the Land of Pleasant Living." Mr. Boh, the brand's iconic one-eyed mascot with a handlebar mustache, is perched atop the Natty Boh Tower overlooking Baltimore. Since 1965, National Bohemian has also been the official sponsor of the Orioles.

When the game ends later that night, Colin drops me off at the Baltimore Greyhound Station for my redeye to New York. After opening the trunk to get my bag, we exchange a

---

[11] The Baltimore Ravens football team is named after *The Raven*, a poem first published by resident Edgar Allen Poe in 1845.

bro-mantic hug goodbye, our final farewell of the summer. As I get ready to walk inside, he retrieves something from the car, and tosses it to me on the curb.

"It's a going-away gift," he announces.

As he shuts his door and drives away, he flashes me a prankster smile through his window. I look down and grimace. *Bastard!* I can't believe what I'm holding in my hand…

A pack of plastic Twizzlers.

A view of the B&O Warehouse behind right field at Camden Yards. Ken Griffey, Jr. is the only person who has ever hit it on the fly.

Colin and I at the *Babe's Dream* statue near the corner of Camden and Eutaw behind center field.

Game 21: Oriole Park at Camden Yards, Baltimore, MD
August 10, 2012 – Royals 1, Orioles 7

Category	Rank	Comments
Best Design	4	In 1992, Camden Yards introduced the first "retro" style ballpark of the modern era.
Best View	10	A hotel and high-rise apartment now block the previous view of the downtown skyline.
Best Hot Dog	18	The $4.75 Essay Hot Dog is very basic, and comes with limited toppings.
Best Mascot	12	*The Oriole Bird* hatched from a giant egg at a game in 1979. It likes to eat the local crab cakes.
Best Fans	25	Although it rained earlier in the day, the attendance was still miserable – 37.6% full on a Friday night.
Best-Looking Females	29	Not too sure – No one showed up!
Best Entertainment	2	Roller coaster cam, "Olé, Olé, Olé, Olé" chant, and a rollerblading saxophonist outside the stadium wearing a Speedo and a pirate hat.
Best Tradition	9	*John Denver's* "Thank God I'm A Country Boy" plays during the Seventh-Inning Stretch, and an "O!" chant traditionally starts the "The Star-Spangled Banner."
Best Feature	8	B&O warehouse on Eutaw Street forms a natural concourse behind right field.
Final Rank	12th	Camden Yards is slightly underrated, because it's the hallmark template of the modern day design.

CHAPTER 25
Miracle on 34ᵗʰ Street

Considering the handful of friends I have in New York City, finding a place to sleep in Manhattan was the least of my worries. Two weeks before I arrived, I e-mailed two friends, hoping I'd get an offer to stay with at least one of them:

Response #1:
Hey man, I wish I could help you out, but I'm actually leaving on vacation to Florida that weekend. Let me know next time you're in town!

Response #2:
Oh man... I'm going to be at a wedding in Maine on August 11, then I head back to SF. Any way you can get here a weekend earlier?

With my two best options out of the question, I then messaged a second tier of friends, one week in advance:

Response #3:
Hey Cody – Sounds like an awesome project! Unfortunately, you're coming to NY the same time I'll be in SoCal for a wedding - terrible timing! :(Good luck with your travels and I'd

love to see the end product!

Response #4:

Hi Cody! I hope you are doing well! I would love to go to the game with you, but that is the worst weekend imaginable for me. I have 2 friends in town and it is also my friends b-day party sat night. If you are going to be in the city you should def come!

Response #5:

I'll call my uncle and see if he's in town. I'm sure he wouldn't mind letting u crash although he's the most annoying person in the world and u may want to kill yourself.

Batting 0-for-5, I turned to Couchsurfing. As it turns out though, New York City is a floodplain of tourists during the summer, spiking demand upon a limited supply. My attempt failed miserably. Then I got desperate, and started reaching out to a few "wild card" acquaintances on Facebook:

Response #6:

Sorry! I'm still at home with my Mom and we don't have space otherwise I would totally invite you over. I just switched jobs, so I'm hoping to work on that soon.

Response #7:

Yeah, he mentioned it. I'm in NC, but my best friend lives there. She doesn't have a couch or even a living room. I'm sort of drunk, I might have some insights in the AM. When is the game?

As I walk into the Baltimore Greyhound Station, I'm face-to-face with the reality that nothing has panned out for New York. In South America, I wouldn't have to worry about an issue like this, but this is different. This is NEW. YORK. CITY. Hotels cost a small fortune.

I approach the ticket counter with a fog of anxiety, my plastic Twizzlers still in hand. For the first time this summer, I'm about to go somewhere without a place to stay. I show the clerk my Discovery Pass.

"I need to go to..." I begin, before trailing off. An idea pops into my head.

"Sir?" she inquires, "What was that?" Seconds of indecision make me feel like a Greyhound tweeker without a home. The woman looks at me like I'm on drugs.

"I need to go to..." I repeat, again cutting myself off. More time passes, her eyes still glaring. Impulsively, I make a split second decision.

"Sorry about that," I announce earnestly. "I'll be going to New Haven, Connecticut."

Minutes later, I'm on the phone with my sister-in-law's family, telling them about the pickle that I've gotten myself into. They live in Milford, one town away from New Haven, and are more than happy to receive me for the weekend.

My last-minute audible is an idea I should've considered earlier. Tomorrow is only Saturday, and I'm not going to the Mets game until Sunday night. This option allows me to spend Saturday and Sunday with family, at the expense of a couple extra hours on the bus. It also buys me another day to figure something out.

In Milford on Saturday afternoon, I hear back from one more person in Manhattan:

Response #8:
Shoot – I think we're too packed in – literally I have two people on the floor of my 400 sq ft studio apartment :((man, timing is shitty. I'm supposed to go rafting/ tubing all day tomorrow too from like 8:30-7 – I totally forgot – if I had more notice I would

have been happy to help out more. :-/

On Sunday morning, I'm well rested and well fed, but nothing else has changed. Prepared to go into battle, I return to the bus station in New Haven. I don't have a place to sleep yet, but I MUST make it to Citi Field tonight. It's the last Mets home game before they go on the road.

When my bus arrives to 8th Avenue and West 42nd in Manhattan, I walk around Times Square and then head south towards Penn Station. I'm glad I've already been to New York three times in my life; otherwise, I'd be completely overwhelmed.

As my anxiety swells among the crowded sidewalk on this summer Sunday afternoon, I decide to turn right at a random intersection. It's much calmer traveling west, and I progress without any destination in mind. After only two blocks, I sit down on the concrete sidewalk with my back pressed against the wall of a brick building. I feel like a junkie who has hit rock bottom. Wandering around is wasting my energy and morale, and I know I need to utilize my strongest muscle – my brain.

The greatest professional skill that I have, besides writing and communicating, is my ability to network. Drawing from my experience in sales, I shed light on a solution by evaluating a new path. *Even though I personally don't know anyone who can host me, I might know someone who knows somebody else, who can.* It's the reference system, and I immediately seek help from my good friend in Miami.

"Heeellooooooo," Kyle answers groggily. He sounds like he has been sleeping on his textbook, which he's known to do on occasion.

I quickly unravel my dire situation. "Do you know

anyone in New York who might be able to put me up for a night or two?" I ask.

"Dude, my ex-girlfriend from high school lives there! I haven't talked to her in forever, but let me call you back real quick."

For the first time, a sparkle of hope reflects off the sidewalk. My phone rings three minutes later, my sanity teetering on the brink.

"I got you a place!" Kyle screams through the phone, now sounding much more awake. I immediately start pumping my fist like an 80's rock band. "I gave Sarah your number," he continues, "She's gonna text you her address."

As soon as Kyle and I hang up, Sarah sends me her address in Brooklyn. I immediately call her back to express my appreciation. While I scrape my body from the sidewalk, I examine a nearby street sign to calculate directions. My jaw drops as I marvel at my supernatural, coincidental location. I had just experienced my own miracle on 34ᵗʰ Street.

Visiting the Jackie Robinson Rotunda inside Citi Field.

Game 22: Citi Field, New York, NY
August 12, 2012 – Braves 5, Mets 6

Category	Rank	Comments
Best Design	26	The Jackie Robinson Rotunda reflects the former design of Brooklyn's Ebbets Field.
Best View	25	Nonexistent and covered in corporate ads.
Best Hot Dog	15	$6.00 Nathan's World Famous Hot Dog is decent, but the condiments take the cake.
Best Mascot	17	*Mr. Met* was baseball's first mascot, but I adamantly dispute he's the best.
Best Fans	24	Meager ESPN Sunday Night Baseball crowd. They booed Chipper Jones every time he came to bat. Rivals – I get it.
Best-Looking Females	30	I wrote this in my notes: "Not cutting it. Well below the average."
Best Entertainment	27	Dunkin' Donuts Cuppy Cam? Party City Dance Cam? *Am I at the roller rink?*
Best Tradition	24	"Meet The Mets" is the signature song played on the radio, TV, and at home games.
Best Feature	9	The Big Apple elevates from a box behind the center field fence after each home run.
Final Rank	29th	The exterior architecture is awesome, modeled after Ebbets Field, but the inside experience lacked heavily.

CHAPTER 26
House That $teinbrenner Built

When I show up to Sarah's apartment in Brooklyn, I find an incredibly friendly and accommodating host. As she shows me around the apartment, she also tells me about her career.

"I work in Tampa every week," she informs me. "I fly out early tomorrow morning, and I'll be staying with my boyfriend tonight. Take the spare key, and feel free to use the apartment however long you want."

An hour ago, I was a bum roaming the street, and now I have an apartment for the week?

As I get ready to leave for the Mets game on ESPN Sunday Night Baseball, I think about Monday night's game at Yankee Stadium. The Texas Rangers visit the Yankees this week in a battle between the American League's best two teams, and I'm worried that ticket prices might skyrocket.

While I organize my belongings, Sarah is in the kitchen texting on her phone. "My coworker just asked me if I want two Yankees tickets for tomorrow," she laughs. "He must've forgot I work with him in Tampa."

My ears perk up like a deer in the woods. "I'll take 'em!" I interject, half-jokingly. "If he can't find someone, tell him you have friend!"

"Really? I'll let him know," she hollers back. "Write down your email for me."

I leave to catch the Subway a few minutes later, saying goodbye to Sarah and thanking her the last-minute hospitality. I catch the "G" train and transfer to the "7", which takes me to Citi Field. As the train approaches the "Mets–Willets Point" stop, I feel my phone vibrate in my pocket. It's a text message from Sarah:

He's emailing you the Yankees tickets for tomorrow. Have fun!

The flags and white "frieze" above upper deck are signature features along the top of Yankee Stadium.

Carrie is one of my Peace Corps friends who I met at the hostel in South America. In preparation for grad school at Columbia, she moved her stuff into an apartment near Yankee Stadium on the morning of the game. So I brought her with me. In the days following, I stayed with her family in upstate New York before we continued on to Canada.

Game 23: Yankee Stadium, New York, NY
August 13, 2012 – Rangers 2, Yankees 8

Category	Rank	Comments
Best Design	25	Modernized version of the original stadium, with amenities, luxuries, and the "Great Hall."
Best View	17	Just a bunch of brick buildings to look at in the Bronx.
Best Hot Dog	24	$5.50 Hebrew National Dog is freshly grilled, but there's only ketchup and mustard at the condiment stand.
Best Mascot	29	The Yankees don't wear names on their jerseys, nor do they have a mascot.
Best Fans	7	Rowdy player chants from right-center field. "Der-ek! Je-ter!" *Clap! Clap! Clap-clap-clap!*
Best-Looking Females	22	There are some good-looking ladies, but I'm not sure if they're actually real baseball fans.
Best Entertainment	18	Smile Cam and puzzle challenges offer weak prizes – A free case of Poland Springs Water? Seriously?
Best Tradition	6	The Yankee Stadium Curtain Call, which I was able to see after Nick Swisher's third inning grand slam.
Best Feature	22	The white "frieze" lining the roof along upper deck is the trademark feature at Yankee Stadium.
Final Rank	23rd	Yankee Stadium is the home of the largest fanbase & most iconic team in baseball.

CHAPTER 27
Molson Country

I return to my seat in the middle of the sixth inning at the Rogers Centre[12], excitedly dreading my $5.25 Stadium Dog. Of the twenty-four ballparks dogs I've purchased and prepped this summer, this one is the most decadent: Salsa, barbeque sauce, chipotle sauce, mustard, jalapenos, onions, relish, and sauerkraut, all stacked on a grilled wiener inside a toasted bun. The condiment stand is no joke in Toronto, and after my first bite, my shirt looks like it has been finger-painted by a two-year-old. My friend Carrie sits next to me, watching in disgust as she gags. In recent weeks, I've had a lot of practice eating hot dogs, and I inhale this particular one like I'm Joey Chestnut at the Coney Island Hot Dog Eating Contest.

Up until this point, my summer has revolved around three core activities: Zigzagging the country like a fugitive, watching baseball, and stuffing my face with "heart attacks on a bun." Physically, I've hardly done any exercise, and I'm starting to feel like I'm stuck inside the fast food documentary, *Super Size Me*.

---

[12] Prior to 2005, Rogers Centre was known as the SkyDome, which opened in 1989.

By the time the seventh inning rolls around, I can almost feel the wiener fat perspiring through my skin. I slouch in my seat and steal a sip of Carrie's Molson beer, feeling AWFUL. If I'm not mistaken, the bad cholesterols are throwing a dance party inside of my arteries. The LDL's are getting hard grinding against the walls of my cardiovascular system. My blood pressure thumps, and without even checking the carotid artery under my jaw, I feel my pulse intensify.

Amid my melodramatic tantrum and miserable state, Carrie comes up with a suggestion. "I know a remedy that'll make you feel better," she teases. "STOP! Eating! HOT DOGS!"

"I have to do it," I stubbornly reply. "It's my thaaang."

Despite my discomfort and craving for an antacid tablet, I know I'm perfectly fine. I'm a healthy twenty-five-year-old who has just gone a little overboard. When I'm in my routine back home, I workout regularly, eat like a bunny, sleep like a princess, and constantly hydrate like I'm recovering from heat stroke. I treat myself like a well-oiled machine, and it's reacting grumpily for putting sludge in the gas tank. Over the past five weeks, I've consumed seventeen ballpark hot dogs to compliment my lack of exercise, horrendous diet, inconsistent sleep, and irregular hydration. My latest meal, the Rogers Centre Stadium Dog, is merely putting me over the top. If I were an old fart, this meal would be the boot that kicks my bucket.

As the seventh inning progresses, I start to feel better as I admire the CN Tower looming overhead. The roof of the dome is open tonight, giving us a perfect view of the 1,814-foot tall behemoth that illuminates the Toronto skyline. Not only is the CN Tower the tallest freestanding structure in the Western Hemisphere, but it's also the fifth tallest in the world[13]. The revolving 360 Restaurant near the top contains the highest wine "cellar" in the world, and completes a full rotation every seventy-two minutes. For those with strong knees, there's also an observation deck with highest glass floor in...

What the...?

In the bottom of the seventh inning, an umpire has halted the course of play. Players stand frozen in shock, the crowd silent. Every fan is wiped with an expression of deep concern.

In the first row of seating along the third base line, an elder gentleman has suffered a heart attack. A member of the medical staff applies rapid chest compressions as another periodically administers mouth-to-mouth. For several minutes, the CPR continues next to the field. White Sox third baseman Kevin Youkilis appears shaken by the scene, along with other players in the vicinity. The victim's wife, wearing an orange top, watches helplessly from the stairs while police stand by her side.

"Where's the AED?" I urgently ask Carrie, referring to an automated external defibrillator. "It should be out there by now. It's been too long."

The medical staff loads the victim on a cart to transport him to the street. One of the staff members, walking along the vehicle, continues to apply chest compressions as it drives across the Astroturf. No AED is in sight, which is unusual at a venue of this magnitude.

Play resumes after four minutes of stoppage, and the crowd sits in a solemn daze as thoughts and prayers go to the

---

[13] The only freestanding structures taller than Toronto's CN Tower are (from tallest to shortest): Burj Khalifa in Dubai, United Arab Emirates; Tokyo Sky Tree in Tokyo, Japan; Abraj Al Bait in Mecca, Saudi Arabia; and Canton Tower in Guangzhou, China.

victim and his family. Besides not utilizing an AED, there's one other thought on my mind: *He must've eaten the Stadium Dog.*

The next morning, I log onto ESPN.com to read the baseball news. One of the headlines stops my heart: *Fan dies following cardiac arrest at Jays Game.*

Among hundreds of comments below the article by readers, two stand out.

> **bjtravgwu:** *Does Rogers Centre not have an AED?*
> AND:
> **sicksense210:** *Those hot dogs are killer.*

Released by the Associated Press, the last line of the article raises a red flag. It reads:

> *This was the second time this season a fan received CPR at a Blue Jays game. It also happened June 29.*

Niagara Falls, which forms a border between the US and Canada, was a must-see stop on the way to Toronto.

There are others who went to multiple games with me, but Carrie was the only one who traveled with me from one location to the next – on the bus. Our day at Niagara Falls and Toronto was the first trip to Canada for the both of us. We loved Canada's favorite coffee shop, Timmy Horton's!

Game 24: Rogers Centre, Toronto, ON
August 16, 2012 – White Sox 7, Blue Jays 2

Category	Rank	Comments
Best Design	28	The "SkyDome" lives up to its original name. It was the first stadium with a fully retractable roof.
Best View	12	If the roof is open, enjoy a sky view of the CN Tower, the world's fifth tallest freestanding structure.
Best Hot Dog	10	The $5.25 Stadium Dog might be so loaded it's lethal – literally. It tastes fantastic though.
Best Mascot	21	Unfortunately, *Ace* the Blue Jay is not on the pitching staff. He also has younger brother, *Junior.*
Best Fans	27	Canadians have a friendly reputation, at least in the summer. Hockey season might be different.
Best-Looking Females	12	I think I have a thing for Canadian girls – I've dated one, and I'd sign up again.
Best Entertainment	26	The "Comfort Cam" exposed oblivious fans lounging in the crowd.
Best Tradition	23	Both the American and Canadian National Anthem is played or performed before every game.
Best Feature	13	The Renaissance Hotel is attached to center field, with seventy rooms overlooking the field of play.
Final Rank	25th	Watching baseball in beautiful Toronto underneath the fifth tallest structure in the world is purely awesome.

CHAPTER 28
Boston (In) Common

Kevin, my hometown friend from Temecula who went with me to Angel Stadium, started his new job in Boston one month ago. I've spent the last four days here, visiting both the Samuel Adams Brewery and the Harpoon Brewery while catching up on sleep.

Kevin and I have tickets tonight for the Tuesday evening matchup between the Angels and Red Sox at Fenway Park[14]. After the game, he's going to drop me off at the Greyhound Station, where I'll catch an overnight bus to Washington D.C.

There's one problem though. Not only does Kevin work all day at his client's office on the outskirts of Boston, but he also lives forty minutes from Fenway Park in the town of Acton. This afternoon, I could potentially ride the commuter rail from Acton to Boston on the "Fitchburg Line", and transfer to the subway for Fenway Park. The issue, however, is that I don't have a way to get from his house to the train station. Taxis don't exist in his neck of the woods, and it's

---

[14] First opened in 1912, Fenway Park celebrated its 100-Year Anniversary during the 2012 season.

much too far to walk.

Since I can't stay at his apartment for the day, we come up with a different solution. Kevin will drop me off at the train station on his way to work this morning, and I'll leave my bag in his car for the day. I'll endure a Bostonian day of tourist activities, and meet him this evening on Lansdowne Street behind the Green Monster, the famous left field wall at Fenway Park. Regardless, this solution still means I have to preoccupy myself in Beantown for next NINE hours...

I arrive on the train to North Station a few minutes before 9:00am. I start my morning with a small Dunkin' Donuts breakfast inside the TD Garden, which connects to the station and serves as the arena for the Boston Celtics. Afterwards, I make my way to Congress Street and head south.

I walk through the New England Holocaust Memorial before I find myself at Faneuil Hall, a historic marketplace and government building that has been a centerpiece in Boston since 1742. As part of the Boston National Historic Park, it's also one of the starting points for tourists exploring the Freedom Trail.

As I'm exploring the gift shops on the first floor, I hear an announcement for a guided walking tour with a park ranger. I've walked the Freedom Trail once before, but I figure the tour will offer free and insightful entertainment. I sign up for it with the sole purpose of killing time.

As my guided tour group exits Faneuil Hall, a husband and wife approach me with a surprising question. "Are you from San Diego?" the man asks.

I look down at my navy blue Padres shirt, and remember that I'm also wearing my San Diego hat. "I am," I reply with a smile.

"So are we!" he exclaims. "We're actually visiting Fenway tonight for the first time."

In between speeches from our guide, I proceed to tell Joey and his wife about my summer of baseball aboard the Greyhound. They love my story and are refreshed to hear it from a Padres fan, particularly since I'm just a few years older than their daughters.

We continue our walk towards the Old State House, where our guide reveals interesting facts about the American Revolution. Boston resident John Adams, a Founding Father and second President of the United States, actually served as defense attorney for the British soldiers following the Boston Massacre.

As our guide continues to detail the public outcry that this caused, Joey leans over and whispers, "Dude, so we went to Cooperstown[15] this weekend. It was awesome!"

"Really?!" I whisper back. "I never had time to make it there. I wanna hear all about it!"

Around noon, we finish our walking tour at the Boston Common, a large park in downtown Boston. As our group disperses, Joey and I pick up our conversation at a deeper level.

"Where about in San Diego are you from?" Joey asks.

"Well, I actually grew up an hour north in Temecula," I mention.

"You're kidding. We LIVE in Temecula!!"

"NOOOO... Really?! What part of town do you live in?"

"We're in Paseo Del Sol," he reveals, referring to a neighborhood just down the road from my house.

After fifteen more minutes of "I-CAN'T-BELIEVE-

---

[15] The National Baseball Hall of Fame and Museum is located in Cooperstown, NY.

THIS!" conversation, Joey and his wife erase the pain of my long afternoon ahead.

"Are you hungry?" Joey asks. "We'd love to have you for lunch. It's our treat."

When I reach Lansdowne Street later that evening, I tell Kevin about my random afternoon with the couple from Temecula. Several days later, I receive a text from a local phone number back home. It reads:

I have given you an Indian name: Cody Thirty Parks. Up for golf when you get back?   - Joey

Kevin (center), his friend Mike (left), and I (right) soaking up the
festivities at Fenway Park.

A young man wearing a Red Sox hat plays the bagpipes on Lansdowne
Street outside Fenway Park. The 'pipes are one of my favorite
instruments, and I love the symbolic simplicity of this photo.

173

Game 25: Fenway Park, Boston, MA
August 21, 2012 – Angels 5, Red Sox 3

Category	Rank	Comments
Best Design	7	Opened in 1912, Fenway Park has the most unusual outfield dimensions in professional baseball.
Best View	23	There isn't a good view of downtown unless you're in the upper deck seats, which still aren't that high.
Best Hot Dog	29	The $5.00 Fenway Frank is horrible. Buy an Italian sausage on Lansdowne Street before the game!
Best Mascot	22	In 1997, *Wally The Green Monster* came out from hiding after fifty years inside the left field wall.
Best Fans	1	Beantown's a rowdy bunch – Fenway Park holds the MLB record for most consecutive sellouts.
Best-Looking Females	8	If you can get past the most unattractive accent in America, hot girls are flocking.
Best Entertainment	7	Arrive early to take part in the fanfare, bagpipers, and sausage vendors on the street outside the ballpark.
Best Tradition	2	*Neil Diamond's* "Sweet Caroline" in the middle of the eighth inning is the most enthusiastic tradition around.
Best Feature	6	The left field fence, *The Green Monster*, is synonymous with the Red Sox.
Final Rank	6th	Between the fans, tradition, and historic setting, watching baseball at Fenway is an unforgettable experience.

CHAPTER 29
Capitol Hill

Following my afternoon tours of the U.S. Capitol Building and the Library of Congress, I walk across the lawn of the National Mall towards the Washington Monument. Between Boston yesterday and D.C. today, I've retained more U.S. history in two days than I did during my entire junior year of high school.

In regard to tonight's game, grey clouds threaten the late afternoon sky. I'm not familiar with weather patterns in this part of the country, but it's dark and unfavorable, the kind of grey that usually doesn't mix well with baseball. When I feel the first drop of water hit my shoulder, I beeline it to the Smithsonian Metro Station and head south towards the ballpark.

Ten minutes later, I arrive to Navy Yard Station, two blocks from Nationals Park. As I ascend up the escalator, the sight of cats and dogs falling from the sky shatters my hope. *It's raining. It's pouring. The old man is snoring...*

When I created the itinerary for my trip, I tried my best not to plan ballpark visits on the last day of a homestand. In the Midwest and East Coast, thunderstorms are prevalent during this time of year, and one rain delay or postponement could ruin my whole trip. Due to scheduling, however, I didn't have a choice in several of the cities; and unfortunately, D.C. is one of them. Similar to my Mets game in New York, tonight is the last game before the Nationals go on the road. In a nutshell, the downpour is threatening to bring my worst summer nightmare to life.

My friend Ashley is here to meet me for the game tonight, and is taking cover from the rain at Justin's Café on First Street. It's one of just a few bars in the area, and is packed with fans escaping the wet weather. From the metro station, I'm forced to sprint the three blocks to the bar.

I haven't seen Ashley since college, so we spend time catching up on our lives and mutual friends once I arrive. Ashley works at the U.S. House of Representatives, and mentions something mid-conversation that I'm shocked I haven't heard of.

"I haven't been to Nationals Park since the Congressional Baseball Game back in June," she says casually.

"Whoa, whoa, back up. What Congressional Baseball Game?" I ask.

As it turns out, the Congressional Baseball Game is an annual charity event played each summer between the Democrats and the Republicans in U.S. Congress. In the old days, the two sides actually had "Republicans" and "Democrats" uniforms, but in the later years, the members switched to individual jerseys that represented professional or college teams from their congressional district or home state.

The Congressional Baseball Game informally began in 1909, and has since become one of Washington's most anticipated events of the year. The game has been held at several venues throughout its history, but has taken place at Nationals Park since in 2008. There have been seventy-nine official games, with forty-one wins for the Republicans, thirty-seven wins for the Democrats, and one tie. Ironically, through 2012, the Democrats have won all four consecutive games since Barack Obama became President. Contrastingly, the Republicans won the previous eight in alignment with George W. Bush's tenure in office. Also interesting is that Ron Paul, who competed against Presidential nominee Mitt Romney in the 2012 Republican Primary Election, was the first player to hit an over-the-fence home run in the Congressional Baseball Game. He did it in 1979, and was elected to the Roll Call Congressional Baseball Hall of Fame in 2012.

On a conclusive note, it's amusing to mention the controversy of the 1913 game. The two teams disputed whether the score should be finalized after the game was stopped in the fourth inning due to rain. By rule in professional baseball, the losing team must bat five full innings for a game to officially count. The Democrats, who were trailing, made their case based on the rule. The Republicans, however, made their case based on the score – They were winning 29-4! This example proves that, NO MATTER WHAT, Democrats and Republicans always have, and always will, find a way to disagree. It's the beauty and the beast of our legal system, demonstrating that there is always a counter argument to anything.

As Ashley and I finish our conversation, the rain comes to a halt as clouds break in the sky. The patrons at the bar make a mass exodus to Nationals Park, and the game starts promptly following a forty-minute delay. When the fifth inning comes to a close, I feel a huge wave of relief as the game becomes "official." The weather holds up for the rest of the night, and immediately after the game, I hop on the bus and fall asleep en route to Florida.

Game 26: Nationals Park, Washington, D.C.
August 22, 2012 – Braves 5, Nationals 1

Category	Rank	Comments
Best Design	10	The Red Porch in center field is one of the biggest restaurants and party decks in baseball.
Best View	19	See views of the U.S. Capitol and Washington Monument from portions of the Upper Deck.
Best Hot Dog	8	$4.75 Nats Dog is okay, but the $7.50 "Half-Smoked, All-The-Way" dog from Ben's Chili is a much yummier tradition.
Best Mascot	6	*Screech* the Bald Eagle is overshadowed by the Presidential mascot race, which takes place in the fourth inning.
Best Fans	12	Good team + US Capital = nearly 30,000 baseball loving fans on a rainy Wednesday.
Best-Looking Females	13	DC's surplus of colleges and young professionals = surplus of attractiveness at Nationals Park.
Best Entertainment	12	The "Presidential Race" features mascots George, Tom, Abe, and Teddy (who won his first race ever on 10/3/12).
Best Tradition	11	Submarine dive horn blares for each home run and win, attributed to the ballpark location at Navy Yard.
Best Feature	23	The grove of Cherry Blossom trees planted behind left field.
Final Rank	11th	I think I've overrated it, but the numbers are hard to argue with. Solid performance in most categories.

C H A P T E R   3 0
Miami, Then Tampa (Errr, St. Petersburg)

Originally, I was supposed to travel from D.C. to
Tampa to go to the Rays game on Friday or Saturday. But I
decided not to do that after getting a persuasive text from Kyle:

*Miami's so sunny and nice right now. Isaac doesn't hit till
Monday, if at all. Plus, it'll be good material if you go through a
hurricane on your trip.*

Convinced by Kyle's plea to come visit him again, I
elect to go to Miami for Friday and Saturday night, postponing
my Rays game until Sunday afternoon. By the time I arrive,
though, Kyle's forecast of "sunny and nice" has circumvented
to "dark and stormy." Regardless, it gives us a couple nights to
hit the club scene like idiots. While fireman-carrying Kyle
across the dance floor on Friday night, two annoying Latina
girls approach us.

The first one asks, "Uhmm… You guys are gayyy,
riiiiight?"

Kyle and I continue pumping our fists. Over the loud
music, I shout back, "Thanks for the compliment! But no,
we're not!"

"Well," the other one continues, "What drugs are you on?"

"We're not!" I emphasize. "We just love each other!"

"Uhmm, so you ARE gay!" the first one insists.

At this point, they still don't get it, so I switch to their native tongue:

"Escucha chicas! No! Somos! Gay! And we're not on drugs either! Now perdón señoritas, es tiempo para mi amigo a bailar en mis hombros!"

As I reflect on the debauchery of Friday night, I'm on my way from Miami to St. Petersburg on the Sunday morning bus. This afternoon's series finale is in a dome, so even though I'm just ahead of Hurricane Isaac, there's no threat for rain at Tropicana Field.

I can't exactly put my finger on it, but something doesn't feel quite right when I arrive to St. Petersburg later that morning. The sky is predictably grey and depressing, but the streets are decrepit. It's like the calm before the storm, but it holds an extra eerie feeling – like I've been transported to the Twilight Zone. This place is a ghost town, and isn't anything like what I've come to expect three hours before a game. Little do I know, but the dreary conditions foreshadow the approaching doom of my ballpark journey.

Tropicana Field is a few blocks from the St. Petersburg bus station, so I have plenty of time to get breakfast before I walk to the game. First though, I step inside the tiny lobby of the Greyhound station to use the restroom. As I pass a TV in the corner, the local sports anchor says something on the news that stops me dead in my tracks: "Here are the highlights of yesterday's rubber game at Tropicana Field..."

Rubber game? A rubber game is the final game that

decides the outcome of a series. *If there's a game today, how is that possible?*

Convinced the TV anchor spoke incorrectly, I stand frozen while I watch the clips of yesterday's game. I fear the worst, but a voice of reason gives me hope. *Baseball teams ALWAYS play on Sunday.*

As the highlight reel finishes, I anxiously await further word. *Surely, he will correct his mistake.* Contrastingly, my heart sinks when he does the opposite:

"In a rare circumstance, the Rays are off today, due to the Republican National Convention being hosted this week at Tropicana Field. They begin a weeklong road trip tomorrow night against the Rangers."

As the words from the TV reach my eardrums and relay to my brain, I stand motionless, without reaction – my face as ghostly as the streets outside. Then, in disbelief, I continue shuffling to the bathroom. I unbuckle my belt, unzip my pants, and stare at the wall above the urinal. *How did I not check the schedule?*

When I come back out to the lobby, I plop down on a bench and check the Rays calendar. As it turns out, the TV man was right – no game. I sit there in shock, in denial that I rearranged my entire weekend under the assumption that there would be a game today. Plus, I was just in Washington, DC! I knew the Republican National Convention started this weekend! For some reason, I thought it was being held in downtown Tampa, not twenty-two miles away at Tropicana Field in St. Petersburg.

Like a frustrated rocket scientist who has overlooked a tiny mistake in a simple formula, I realize I've made an error that a rookie fan would never make – I FORGOT TO LOOK AT THE SCHEDULE. A blank stare overtakes my face as I look out a window for the next thirty minutes. My mind ticks.

If I stay in Florida until the Rays come back, it interferes with my last three stops. Putting three in jeopardy as a sacrifice for one doesn't make sense. That aside, a misfortunate fact plays through my head: *Of the fifteen teams hosting a series this weekend, this is the only one that doesn't have a Sunday game.*

Frustrated and aloof, I seek guidance from my fellow ballpark guru. Colin replies to my text confession with a simple message:

That sucks. Tampa blows anyway. Skip it.

After I finally come to terms that I've made a critical mistake, I'm left with no choice but to forget about it. A bad mood doesn't change what has already happened; in fact, I should probably feel blessed that this is the first bad experience of my summer. Without looking back, I board the next bus heading north, happy to escape the hurricane-depressed streets of St. Petersburg. As we cruise along the Gulf of Mexico, one thing is for certain… This just became a twenty-nine-park tour.

Ashley (middle), her friend Mike (left), and I enjoying drier conditions during the Nationals game in Washington DC.

CHAPTER 31
Lone Ranger

I had always wanted to visit the French Quarter in New Orleans, so I made plans to stay there for a night on my way to Texas. But when my bus arrived in the bayou at 8:00am Monday morning, everyone in the gulf region was boarding up their windows, in fear that Katrina's angry cousin was gonna beat 'em with a rainstick. The line of evacuees outside of the New Orleans bus terminal reminded me of Best Buy on Black Friday. I was worried that if I got off the bus, I might never be able to get back on. I immediately changed my plans, stayed onboard, and kept riding west. Last night, after the all day ride from NOLA, I finally arrived in Austin, Texas.

It's already time to get moving again as I wake this morning at my friend's apartment. I'm making a quick trip to Dallas for the Rangers game tonight, and am leaving most of my belongings here since I'll be back tomorrow afternoon. Tonight, I'll be staying with my friend Andrew, who was my "Big Bro" in my college fraternity. He and his girlfriend (also a college friend) just moved to Dallas, and they're excited to welcome their first visitor.

The Dallas-Ft. Worth area is a massive, sprawling metropolis that presents itself as a massive, sprawling problem when you don't have a car. Rangers Ballpark in Arlington is eighteen miles west of Dallas, which means I have eighteen miles to go when I arrive to the downtown Greyhound station. Andrew might be able to pick me up in a few hours, but he's not sure if he'll be off work in time for the game. I can't risk it, so I start exploring alternative ways to get there for as cheaply as possible. This will be a game of *Cowboys and Indians*, and I will be the Lone Ranger pressing west across eighteen miles of unknown frontier.

My first thought is a local bus, but I quickly discover there aren't any buses in, or to, Arlington. Texas is an oil state, and a big state full of oil means a big state full of self-reliant drivers, which in turn, is a big state with limited public transit. The sum of all this only means one thing: I'm S.O.L.

The Lone Ranger then discovers DART (Dallas Area Rapid Transport), a metro train that serves the greater Dallas region. The Blue Line runs between downtown and Ft. Worth, and makes a stop seven miles north of the ballpark. Not that convenient, but it's a start.

Upon further research, I also find out that the City of Arlington has a free trolley shuttle that makes numerous stops at local hotels, Cowboys Stadium, Six Flags Over Texas, and Rangers Ballpark in Arlington. The nearest hotel in the trolley loop is only four-and-a-half miles from the DART stop at Centreport/DFW Airport, cutting off two-and-a-half miles of travel. If I can find a way to get from my DART stop to the Admiral Hotel in Arlington, then my problem is solved.

As I ride westward on the DART train, I look out the window and reflect on the past seven days. I've been to Fenway Park in Boston, inside the U.S. Capitol Building in Washington, on dance floors in Miami, to the ghost town of St. Petersburg, to the mass exodus in New Orleans, to a barbeque restaurant in Austin, and now, on the modern-day Pony Express in Dallas. I'm worn out, and it's no wonder why; by the time I finally reach the Ballpark in Arlington this afternoon, I'll have ridden 2,767 miles (the long way) just to get from my twenty-sixth ballpark to my twenty-seventh. If MTV documented this, the show would likely be called *True Life: I'm A Ballpark Psycho*.

When I step off the train at the Centreport DART stop, I find free shuttles servicing Dallas-Ft. Worth Airport to the north, but nothing to the south. There aren't any cabbies standing by, so I call a taxi company and wait by the curb. Within ten minutes, a driver arrives to pick me up. I tell him I need to go to the Admiral Hotel, and we begin driving the four-and-a-half miles south.

The man behind the wheel is a friendly middle-eastern guy named Bob. He looks like someone I'd expect to see in Manhattan, but his personality is a product of the South. He says "God Bless" when he hangs up the phone, which sounds oddly bizarre through his accent. Despite being an immigrant, it's evident that Bob is westernized. Or, as I like to call it, Texanized.

My Mom's entire side of the family lives in the Lone Star State, and because of my bloodline, I keep an English-to-Texan translation guide on my bookshelf at home. When I say that Bob is Texanized, what it really means is that the following definitions have been accepted into everyday life:

House Pet = Armadillo
Bank Machine = Oil Rig
Sun Block = Cowboy Hat
Night Out = A Barbeque and A Park Bench
Champagne = Lone Star Beer
Snack = Road Kill

Security System = Rifle

And in Bob's case: Goodbye = God Bless.

Next to Bob in the passenger seat is an extremely elder foreign man wearing a finely woven cowboy hat atop his hairless head. He and his Fu Manchu moustache rest silently while Bob talks on the phone. When Bob hangs up, curiosity gets the best of me.

"Hey Bob, is this your Dad?" I ask.

"This guy?" Bob responds, pointing at Mr. Fu Manchu. "I have no idea who he is. I just found him on the street when I was coming to pick you up. He doesn't speak English. He just handed me this."

I lean forward to retrieve an 8.5" x 11" piece of paper from Bob's hand. One giant word is written across the middle in permanent marker: *ECONOLODGE*. From living and traveling in Asia, I recognize that the handwriting has Japanese characteristics. I take a closer look at Bob's front seat passenger, and things become much more clear. Lone Ranger is riding alongside a Japanese cowboy. He could be Ichiro's sensei for all I know. *Yee-haw!* And our cattle driver is a middle-eastern gent named Bob. *This is starting to feel a lot more like the Silk Road than the Santa Fe Trail.*

When we arrive to the Admiral Hotel, I give Bob twenty dollars and hop out of the van before things get any more weird. I walk inside to find a sign by the door informing shuttle passengers that they must have a ticket. I approach a lovely looking lady behind the desk.

"Hi, is this where I get a shuttle ticket for the ballpark?" I inquire.

"Sure is. What's your room number?" she asks.

"Oh, I'm not a guest. I just cabbed here to ride the shuttle," I admit.

"Actually, the shuttle is for hotel guests only…"

"Really?" I respond, almost rudely. "Are you serious?"

Like a flashback of my life at the moment of my death, I reflect on all the hoops I've jumped through over the past several days to get here. The picture on my face is worth a thousand bad words. As I think of a way to convey my desperation, she throws me a bone.

"Wait! You're the gentleman in Room 147, right? I'm so sorry." A confused look sweeps across my face before I catch on to her playful drift.

She hands me a pass, and after 2,765 miles, I relish in the last two aboard the free Arlington trolley. As I approach my twenty-seventh ballpark of the trip, I think about the sign in Baltimore hanging above the whiskey bar at *The Horse You Came In On*:

Life should not be a journey to the grave with the intention of arriving safely in a pretty and well preserved body, but rather to skid in broadside, thoroughly used up, totally worn out, and loudly proclaiming, "WOW, WHAT A RIDE!"

Yeah, this Lone Ranger couldn't agree more.

Lone Ranger's ride was unnecessary. Andrew came in the first inning.

Game 27: Rangers Ballpark in Arlington, Arlington, TX
August 28, 2012 – Rays 0, Rangers 1

Category	Rank	Comments
Best Design	24	Has Texas-style stone carvings and an outer facade made of brick and Sunset Red granite.
Best View	27	Four-story offices built into center field enclose the park from exterior views.
Best Hot Dog	13	$4.50 Jumbo Dog is good, but I triple-dog-dare you to try the two-foot long, one-pound, $26 "Boomstick" with shredded cheese, chili, onions, jalapenos, and fries.
Best Mascot	20	*Rangers Captain* is a palomino-style horse that dresses variably to match the uniforms.
Best Fans	13	30,700 Tuesday night fans signify the revival of the Rangers over the past few seasons.
Best-Looking Females	5	The GRITS are served hot in Dallas. GRITS = "Girls Raised In The South."
Best Entertainment	17	*Soulja Boy's* "Crank That" blares loudly when "Yuuuuuuuuuuuu" Darvish takes the mound.
Best Tradition	21	The song "Deep In The Heart Of Texas" plays in the middle of the fifth inning.
Best Feature	24	*Greene's Hill* is the iconic section of sloped grass behind the center field fence.
Final Rank	20th	Rangers Ballpark has Texas fanfare and a design found nowhere else, but it has become dated compared to other venues.

CHAPTER 32
Houston, We Have A Problem

On the Friday before Labor Day weekend, I backtrack to Houston to visit my aunt, uncle, and cousins. One of my cousins and I go out to a bar that night, where a fellow patron makes the most ridiculous drink order I've ever seen.

"Shots for the whole bar!" the guy demands, handing his credit card to the bartender.

The bartenders proceed to pour seventy-eight shots, one for each person in the establishment. The entire bar takes the shot together, and immediately afterwards, the same guy makes the second most ridiculous drink order I've ever seen.

"One more round!!" he shouts to the bar staff.

The bartenders refill all seventy-eight shot glasses, and everyone throws back another. Collectively, we have consumed 156 shots in five minutes. Cheers, mate. You just wasted your money.

After going to the Astros game the next night with my family, my cousin and I head down to the gulf on Sunday afternoon. Her friend's boyfriend has a beach house in Surfside, and has invited a bunch of us down for the night. When we get there, it turns into an afternoon of swimming, tossing the pigskin, drinking beer, and barbecuing. In

California, this would be the perfect day, but at this particular location in Texas, it's pretty cotton-pickin' miserable. The air outside is more humid than my armpit, and mosquitoes are feasting on me like my corpse decomposed a week ago. Some of the houses near the beach remind me of the Amazon village shacks I saw in the springtime. They stand on wooden stilts above a dried up floodplain, without air conditioning to seek refuge from the swamp. I'm not sure which day of the week God created hurricanes, but I'm confident he invented them to prevent humans from settling at hell-on-Earth places such as this.

After a full day of sweating dried salt and slapping mosquitoes off my sunburned calves, I step into the most disgusting shower of my life at 9:15pm. As more mosquitoes buzz around black mold on the ceiling, I adjust the water temperature to cold – ice cold. I can feel sweat and sand and salt and beer beading off my skin as I wash myself. And even though I've been drinking for six hours straight, I don't feel buzzed in the slightest. I think I've perspired out every drop of alcohol that I've consumed.

As I've already mentioned, the houses here are on stilts, so the living area is actually on the second level. There's a rickety staircase on the side of this house that leads from the ground level up to a wooden balcony outside the front door. Inside, the living room, kitchen, and guest room feel just as sticky as the outside, minus the bloodsucking leg chompers. The master bedroom does have air conditioning though, and fortunately, my cousin and I have already set up an air mattress on the floor. Claiming this spot is clutch considering that thirteen people are sleeping here tonight.

When I turn off the water and step out of the shower, I hear everyone talking and drinking out on the balcony, which is on the other side of the bathroom wall. It's probably about 9:30 now, which gives me fifteen minutes until the taxis arrive to take us to some bar that I pray has air conditioning. Despite my cold shower, the bathroom feels like a sauna, which is disgusting to get dressed in when you're still sweating. I do it quickly though, eager to catch up outside.

As I reach for the door handle to exit the bathroom, I hear a thunderous crash on the other side. I yank the door open, but step into silence. To my right, I notice the front door is wide open, and as I look down, disbelief glares through my eyes. The balcony is gone!

As I approach the doorframe, which is now an open ledge operating as a second level window, I gaze down upon the ground below. Amid the darkness, I see a white PVC pipe splattered with blood, and traces of silent bodies sprawled in shock. Only one thought crosses my mind: *Houston, we have a problem.*

I quickly realize I'm the only person remaining in the house, and that everyone else has gone down with the balcony, including my cousin. She has landed on top of somebody else, and appears to be unharmed. A few people start helping others who are more seriously hurt. No one appears to be dead.

I rush back inside the bathroom to retrieve towels and First Aid supply, and then toss it down to the victims. One girl is now sitting on the bottom step of the remaining staircase, with the entire left side of her head covered in blood. It's dripping down her neck. She presses a towel against her head to minimize the bleeding, and then hops in a taxi with two friends to go to the hospital.

In the aftermath, I notice that my cousin's best friend has split open the underside of her chin, and has blood dripping down her Adam's apple. Her boyfriend loads her in his car, while several other friends, including my cousin, climb in the backseat to go with them. It's like the buddy system when ladies use the restroom – whether or not you need to go, everyone's going to the hospital. I'm all in favor of the support, but the next thing I know, everyone's gone, and I'm still stranded on the second level of the house. All. By. Myself.

In the back of my mind, there's a slight fear that the whole house might collapse, but I decide to accept the risk over the mosquitoes outside. The good news is that the beer coolers are in the house, so I crack open a cold one and take a seat in the middle of the living room. Suddenly, as a ladder appears and a body comes crawling through a window, I realize one other person has stayed behind. As luck would have it, it's the autistic brother of some guy who arrived when I was in the shower. The other guy went to the hospital when his girlfriend got hurt, and left his disabled brother behind. In the dark. With a ladder. And me. *No problem bro. I'll play camp counselor.*

I drink beer the rest of the night as I repeatedly answer the same questions over and over again. My new friend drills me with his biographical interrogation, pretending to be a clandestine CIA agent. I'm forced to tell him about the breed of my dogs, the ages of my siblings, my high school mascot, my birthday horoscope, the sports I played in high school, my middle name, my favorite color, my second favorite color, my favorite dessert, my favorite Mario Kart 64 characters. He absolutely picks me apart. As it continues to carry on, I sit in a chair with my hand supporting the side of my head. One thought is still rolling through my brain: *Houston, we have a problem.*

Junction Jack is legit. He is/was the real team mascot! No phony BS.

My Uncle Mark stitched together a panoramic shot from our seats at
Minute Maid Park.

Game 28: Minute Maid Park, Houston, TX
September 1, 2012 – Reds 1, Astros 2

Category	Rank	Comments
Best Design	12	The historic Union Station train depot was maintained and rebuilt as the left field wall.
Best View	20	Facing northwest, downtown is out of sight, although a few buildings are in view.
Best Hot Dog	19	The $4.75 Star Dog is hotly rotated with onions, relish, and jalapenos as condiment options.
Best Mascot	26	*Junction Jack* is a semi-retired railroad engineer. With the move to the AL West in 2013, Orbit (from the Astrodome) will return.
Best Fans	29	College Football Saturday + Worst record in baseball = Very tame audience in Astroland.
Best-Looking Females	27	Houston barely makes the cut for top three most attractive cities in Texas (i.e. Austin & Dallas)
Entertainment	3	Displaying preoccupied fans on their smart phones, the "Oblivious Cam" is a classic.
Best Tradition	10	Life-size train filled with oranges steams down 800 feet of track after each home run.
Best Feature	1	*Tal's Hill* is a grassy slope in center field with a flagpole in the field of play.
Final Rank	18th	My favorite of the retractable roof stadiums. *Tal's Hill* and the locomotive train are wildly interesting.

CHAPTER 33
Take Me Out With The Crowd

If anyone is wondering where the money sleeps in our country, the answer is blatantly disguised across baseball. Thirteen of the thirty ballparks are represented by just three business categories in our economy. Great American Ballpark, Progressive Field, and Safeco Field all hold naming contracts with insurance companies. In the beverage sector, Busch Stadium, Coors Field, and Miller Park represent beer brands, while Minute Maid Park and Tropicana Field constitute the juice industry. Lastly, Citi Field, Citizens Bank Park, Comerica Park, PNC Park, and Chase Field round out the list of ballparks named after banking firms.

Historically, baseball is a sport played and followed by men. As a man myself, it's easy to understand the marketing philosophy behind the ballpark naming contracts. Men drive cars (and need insurance). Men drink beer (as noted in Chapter 11). And men like money (well, women like money, so men need a place to hide it). In Phoenix, my last stop of the trip, I'm again reminded of the corporate sponsorships across baseball designed to infiltrate consumer psychology. Chase Field is named on behalf of one of the largest and most recognizable financial institutions in the country.

On the eleventh of September, I stand up during the Seventh Inning Stretch in Arizona. This is my thirtieth rehearsal[16] this summer of *Take Me Out To The Ballgame*, which is also my three-year-old niece's favorite song. As I recite the lyrics, I record a video on my phone, and send it to my sister-in-law to share with her.

As I've just noticed though, the Diamondbacks are another one of the many teams in baseball that have yet to figure out the lyrics to *Take Me Out To The Ballgame*. Earlier this summer, I complained to Colin about the inconsistency of the lyrics at several other ballparks around the country. As I've progressed on my trip, I've become baffled by the number of teams that display the incorrect words on the jumbotron during the middle of the seventh inning. To me, it's disrespectful to the history of the song, and disrespectful to the history of the game. And the discrepancy isn't within one line; there are inconsistencies in three different places! I'll illustrate my point with the following examples:

In Line 2, which is correct?
"Take me out *to* the crowd."
Or:
"Take me out *with* the crowd."

In line 4, which is correct?
"I don't care if I *ever* get back,"
Or:
"I don't care if I *never* get back,"

---

[16] Remember: I went to two games in Cincinnati, but missed the game in Tampa.

And in line 5, which is correct?
"*For it's* root, root, root for the home team,"
Or:
"*Let me* root, root, root for the home team,"

In all three examples, the second option is correct. Not to pick on the Diamondbacks, but the lyrics on their video board reads, "I don't care if I *ever* get back." In Kansas City, the Royals make the same mistake, and in New York, the Mets display, "*We will* root, root, root for the home team." Busch Stadium in St. Louis has errors, too. These are only the few places where I consciously paid attention, but I'd venture to estimate that nearly half of the ballparks botch at least one word.

For the official record, *Take Me Out To The Ballgame* was authored by Jack Norworth and composed by Albert Von Tilzer, neither of whom had *ever* (or *never?*) been to a baseball game when the song was originally released in 1908. The modern-day version that fans sing during the seventh inning is actually the original chorus. The first and second verses have been omitted for simplicity.

The truth is that the finale of my tour is mostly anticlimactic. My bus pass expired as soon as I arrived in Phoenix, and my visit to Chase Field goes as planned. As I've progressed on my journey, though, the lyrical inconsistency of *Take Me Out To The Ballgame* has developed into one of my major pet peeves (as well as hat-wearing during *God Bless America*). For anyone who cares about the conservation of our national pastime, it's our duty as fans to stir demand for its restoration at our home ballparks. It's important for children like my niece to learn it correctly, so it continues to be a baseball tradition for generations to come.

I stayed with my Uncle Doug and Darleen during my visit to Phoenix. Our seats at Chase Field were one of the best spots I had all summer.

Chase Field has a pool and a jacuzzi behind the right-center field fence. Now that's baseball paradise!

Game 29: Chase Field, Phoenix, AZ
September 11, 2012 – Dodgers 0, Diamondbacks 1

Category	Rank	Comments
Best Design	22	First U.S. ballpark with a retractable roof, and one of only two ballparks (Detroit) with a dirt "keyhole" strip from the mound to home plate.
Best View	28	Sweltering heat forces the retractable roof shut, limiting an already limited view.
Best Hot Dog	23	$5.50 D-backs Dog isn't grilled or toasted, and only comes with basic toppings.
Best Mascot	23	*D. Baxter* is a bobcat because Chase Field used to be known as "The BOB."
Best Fans	26	The rowdiest baseball in Arizona happens in March during Spring Training.
Best-Looking Females	11	Like the weather, desert girls are hot.
Best Entertainment	25	The $14 million scoreboard above center field is the fifth largest high-definition screen in baseball.
Best Tradition	19	The Legends Mascot Race: Mark Grace v. Randy Johnson v. Matt Williams v. Luis Gonzalez.
Best Feature	10	The private pool and Jacuzzi behind the fence in right-center field.
Final Rank	28th	Chase Field is a cool baseball park in a hot desert. I'd rank it much higher if everyone was allowed to swim in the pool.

CHAPTER 34
My Rally Cap

Are you kidding? Do I seem like the type of person who would have the audacity to write an entire book about thirty ballparks but only visit twenty-nine? Who do you think I am? Someone who has "failure" in my vocabulary? Never heard of it. I'll be damned if I get this far and not finish what I've started.

My spirit does not believe in "almost", "could have", or "next time." It operates with a fight-till-you-die attitude of perseverance, determination, and achievement. In pursuit of my dream, the hide-and-go-seek character inside of me screams, "Ready or not Tampa, here I come!!!"

Three days after flying from Phoenix to California on the non-refundable ticket that I untimely booked the night before I missed the game in St. Petersburg, my Dad returns me to the airport for another round. The good news is that my Old Man has bailed me out of an expensive flight by redeeming his frequent flyer miles on my behalf. The bad news is that we booked the ticket on short notice, so I'll be flying redeye tonight from San Jose to LAX to Newark to Tampa, and then returning from Tampa forty-eight hours later via Houston to Phoenix and back to San Jose. As the phrase goes, *you get what you pay for...* And I haven't paid for a thing.

While I'm waiting at the airport, I find out through Facebook that Steve, my Couchsurfing friend who brought me to the Braves game in Atlanta, will also be in Tampa during the next two days. He's there for a medical research conference, so we make plans to go to the Rays game on Thursday evening.

When I arrive to Tampa on Wednesday morning, my college friend and host, Ben, is swamped with clinical rotations as a third-year medical student at USF. He doesn't have any free time during my visit, but lives conveniently close to Steve's hotel. On Thursday afternoon, Steve picks me up in his rental car, and the two of us embark on the twenty-two-mile trek to Tropicana Field. As each mile passes by, I'm left wondering how I would've made it to this game if it weren't for Steve's coincidental timing. After all the incredible blessings I've had this summer, I take this one with a grain of salt, knowing my fate is in the hands of the baseball gods. Like a Greek warrior, they're probably watching over me from their heavenly thrones at Elysian Fields.

A massive sigh of relief lifts from my shoulders as Steve and I enter Tropicana Field, my unlikely thirtieth and final ballpark of the journey. We immediately visit the Rays Touch Tank, where fans are able to dip their hands into a 10,000-gallon saltwater tank to pet real cownose rays behind the right field fence. After drying my hands off, I take a picture of the rays with the field in the background, and post the photo on Facebook. Several minutes later, my friend Phil offers the following comment:

> *Look at how many fun things they can do in that tank! They should have a ray for every player in the Rays organization; if a player is released, they release the ray into the ocean. If a player is*

traded, the trade should stipulate that the acquiring team must care for the ray at their facility. If a player dies an unexpected death, the ray must die as well. And if a player gets suspended, the ray gets put on time-out in a separate tank.

As Steve and I laugh it up, we exit the Rays Touch Tank to check out the rest of the ballpark. He then casually mentions a very appealing tidbit of information.

"Oh, I forgot to tell you. When I travel for work, I have a one hundred dollar food allowance per day. And I haven't touched it yet."

After telling me this, Steve and I raid the concession stand near our seats in the upper deck. When we finally sit down, we have enough food to feed an army. I feel like Billy Heywood in the movie *Little Big League*. In my tray alone, I'm carrying a Kayem Heater Dog smothered with chili and cheese, a large order of chili cheese fries, and two large beers. By the fourth inning, I'm as uncomfortable as I was in Toronto.

I'm back to feeling better by the time the seventh inning rolls around, and have become friends with a lady sitting near us celebrating her birthday. She's also the ringleader of the "Left-Right Club", a verbally heckling, cowbell-ringing group of season ticket holders. Anytime a Rays opponent strikes out, members of the Left-Right Club scream, "Left! – Right! – Left! – Right! – Left! – Right!" in synchronized unison as the player takes each step back to the bench. Then, when the player reaches the top step of the dugout, they scream, "Sit down!!" It's the most original and consistent heckling chant I've witnessed all summer, and it's especially effective with David Price[17] on the mound tonight. Furthermore, I'm

---

[17] David Price won the 2012 American League Cy Young Award after pitching his way to a 20-win season and a career-best 2.56 ERA.

impressed by the initiative this woman has taken to establish the organization as an underground cult. I feel included in their special society when she hands me an honorary membership card.

As the end of the game approaches, I consider it ironic that Florida, a state I had never been to prior to 2012, is the setting of both my first and last game of the tour. Every visit this year has coincided with the occurrence of something unordinary, such as the improbable, come-from-behind, walk-off grand slam in Miami, the presence of Hurricane Isaac, and the Republican National Convention. As the game moves to the bottom of the ninth inning, I wonder if my streak of strange events has finally come to an end. But with three outs remaining and the Rays losing 4-1, perhaps the table is set for one more act of magic. Unlike my game in Miami, none of the fans are leaving early.

In an episode of déjà vu, the bottom of the ninth unfolds in similar fashion to my first game way back on the thirteenth of May. Matt Joyce singles. Jeff Keppinger singles. Luke Scott sacrifices the runners to second and third. Carlos Pena follows with an RBI single. It's now 4-2 with one out, and two men on base.

Stephen Vogt then walks, loading the bases. With the crowd buzzing in anticipation, Desmond Jennings hits a single to center field, knocking in the two tying runs. With an otherwise dormant game suddenly energized in a 4-4 tie, Red Sox manager Bobby Valentine decides to go to his bullpen.

With the score even and a new pitcher taking the mound, the scenario feels all too familiar. It's a nostalgic reminder of the plays that occurred leading up to Giancarlo Stanton's walk-off grand slam for the Marlins. As chills shoot through my spine, wishful thinking challenges conventional rationale. *Could it be possible, that the first and last games of my tour, both strangely in Florida, end with climatic walk-off home runs? Coincidences like that only happen in storybooks…*

As B.J. Upton steps inside the batter's box, I flashback to a crappy poem that I published in high school, titled *Mr. Clutch*:

He drowns out the crowd,
Isolates his thoughts,
Feels his every heartbeat,
Imagining the magic once again.

Relaxing his mind,
He cradles the lumber in his palm,
Digs deeper in the box
The fans roar.

A white rocket shoots through timeless air,
Like the release of a triggered gun.
He envisions every seam,
A blur of red on white attacks,
He counters with a quick swing.

The ball sails deep and beyond,
Roars of thunder erupt,
Flashes of lightning strike,
A wave of triumph perseveres
From one swing of the bat.

Suddenly he snaps out of his fog,
Prepares to deliver for the faithful.
It is time now,
Time to come through in the clutch.

Exactly at that moment, on the first pitch of the at-bat, the fairytale comes to life. As I watch my daydream become reality, time nearly stops as my endorphins fire at a record high. Lightning has struck twice.

As B.J. Upton's three-run, walk-off home run carries 416 feet over the center field fence, every part of me knows that this was how my summer was supposed to end. Life works in mysterious ways sometimes, and so does baseball. I reflect on all the changes and decisions and turns I've made in my life, and recognize that the culmination of my choices has led me to be right here, right now, at the pinnacle of my journey. After taking a leap of faith twelve months ago when I left Los Angeles, I'm accepting tonight's dramatic finish as a sign from God that I've listened for my calling, followed my heart, and found the path where I am meant to be. What I do from here on out remains to be seen, but for right now, I am living my dream and following my destiny. I have made the most of my *30 Tickets To Paradise*.

My honorary membership card to the "Left-Right Club."

Dipping my hand in the water to pet a cownose ray. You know you've found baseball paradise when SeaWorld comes to the ballpark!

The Rays Touch Tank is a 10,000-gallon saltwater aquarium that sits behind the right-center field fence at Tropicana Field.

Game 30: Tropicana Field, St. Petersburg, FL
September 20, 2012 – Red Sox 4, Rays 7

Category	Rank	Comments
Best Design	30	Odd lighting, small dimensions, and a catwalk hanging from the top of the dome that occasionally gets hit by fly balls.
Best View	30	It's a permanent dome. No view.
Best Hot Dog	11	Chili and cheese is stacked on the $7.00 Kayem Heater Dog. I felt the "heat" an hour later.
Best Mascot	13	According to the Rays website, *Raymond* is a blue fuzzy "Canus Manta Whatthefluffalus."
Best Fans	28	The cowbell-ringing *Left-Right Club* holds down the fort in the upper deck section behind home plate.
Best-Looking Females	25	I know Florida has some chicas, but I doubt you'll find many at Trop. Try spring training instead.
Best Entertainment	30	Tropicana Field feels like a theme park circus, with a Pepsi bottle race as the highlight act.
Best Tradition	13	Tropicana's roof is lit in orange after every Rays win, resembling the peeled fruit.
Best Feature	3	The Rays Touch Tank is a 10,000-gallon petting zoo behind the fence in right-center field.
Final Rank	27th	Not sure how Trop didn't finish last next to Oakland, but I sort of fell in love with the Rays Touch Tank. I love animals.

CHAPTER 35
My Box Score

Since returning home to California, I've compiled a summary of statistics, events, and fun facts that I did *not* cover in the storyline. The following list of thirty items is a "box score" of my summer:

1) The home team won 20 of the 31 games I attended.

2) I saw the Padres, Dodgers, Twins, and Braves play four times each. And the Dodgers never won!

3) My highest scoring game was played on July 16th at Target Field in Minneapolis. The Twins beat the Orioles by a score of 19-7, and the two teams combined for 33 hits.

4) At U.S. Cellular Field on July 24th, the White Sox and Twins combined for five home runs, most of any game I attended.

5) The longest game I attended lasted 3 hours, 55 minutes at Busch Stadium in St. Louis. The Cardinals won that game 3-2 in 12 innings on July 25th.

6) My longest game was also the hottest. For the first pitch, it was 102 degrees (plus humidity) at Busch Stadium at 7:00pm.

7) I witnessed two grand slams, the first being Giancarlo Stanton's walk-off in Miami on May 13th. The other happened exactly three months later, on August 13th, when Nick Swisher did it in the third inning at Yankee Stadium against the Rangers. Four batters later, with the bases loaded again, Curtis Granderson nearly hit the second grand slam of the inning for the Yankees, but the ball was caught on the warning track in center field.

8) San Francisco and Detroit, which played each other in the 2012 World Series, had the second and third largest crowds of all the games I attended, respectively. Yankee Stadium had the highest mark with 45,676 fans. Philadelphia, which had the fourth largest crowd of my tour, had the highest total attendance of any city throughout the 2012 season.

9) I only spent $2,563.18 during the entire trip, which included my game tickets, gas, flights, bus pass, public transportation, food, drinks, and miscellaneous expenses.

10) I was given a free ticket, or brought to a game as a guest, at ten different ballparks. These cities were San Francisco, Kansas City, Milwaukee, Atlanta, Cincinnati, Cleveland, Pittsburgh, New York (Yankees), Houston, and Phoenix.

11) Thanks to a generous group of friends, family, and Couchsurfing hosts, I never once had to pay for accommodation. They all fed me, too.

12) I spent the night in 56 different places over the 131 days from my first game to my last. During this time, I visited 37 U.S. states, plus the Canadian province of Ontario.

13) I paid $564 for the 60-Day Discovery Pass. Greyhound discontinued selling this unlimited travel package as of September 30, 2012.

14) I spent 256.5 hours (nearly 11 full days) riding the bus a total of 11,492 miles, which accrued to a cost of $0.04 per mile. To compare the distance, this would be the same as driving 46% of the Earth's circumference along the Equator.

15) I spent $157.25 on ballpark hot dogs.

16) There aren't any new stadiums in the process of being built. I predict the Oakland A's will be the next team to move into a new park, but for now, I have no worries about my trip becoming outdated in the near future.

17) Let it be known that I am *not* a relative of Ewing Kauffman, the founder of the Kansas City Royals whom their ballpark is named after.

18) Outfielder Reed Johnson, who played for both the Cubs and Braves in 2012, graduated from my high school ten years before me. Alternatively, Allen Craig of the St. Louis Cardinals went to my rival high school.

19) When the Cleveland Indians lost to the Twins at Progressive Field on August 6th, it broke my streak of nine consecutive wins by the home team.

20) Chicago White Sox owner Jerry Reinsdorf has owned the Chicago Bulls since 1985.

21) Prior to every game, the Atlanta Braves ticket office sells $1.00 seats for a designated section in the right field upper deck on a first-come, first-served basis. They are not available for online purchase.

22) The Cincinnati Reds officially changed their name to the "Redlegs" from 1956–1960. With the onset of McCarthyism and the Red Scare of the 1950's, the

owners altered the nickname to disassociate the team from Communism.

23) After the Dodgers and Giants moved from New York to California following the 1957 season, the New York Mets adopted Dodger blue and Giants orange when they became an expansion team in 1962. They played their first two seasons at the Polo Grounds, the former home of the New York Giants.

24) 2012 marked the final season the Houston Astros played in the National League Central Division. With their move to the American League West, both leagues now have fifteen teams. By default, balancing the leagues with an odd number of teams creates a scheduling situation that forces interleague play during all stages of the season.

25) The Boston Red Sox, New York Yankees, and San Francisco Giants are the only three teams in baseball that do not display player names on the back of their *home* uniforms.

26) Surprisingly, only twelve teams have home dugouts on the third base side. The list includes the Arizona Diamondbacks, Chicago Cubs, Chicago White Sox, Cleveland Indians, Detroit Tigers, Los Angeles Angels of Anaheim, Los Angeles Dodgers, Miami Marlins, Oakland A's, Pittsburgh Pirates, San Francisco Giants, and Toronto Blue Jays. The other eighteen teams all occupy the first base side at home.

27) I visited five breweries along the way: Mission Brewery in San Diego, Redhook Brewery near Seattle, Miller Brewing Company in Milwaukee, Samuel Adams in Boston, and Harpoon Brewery in Boston.

28) Good news: I was able to visit Niagara Falls and ride the *Maid Of The Mist* boat. I got soaked. Bad news: I didn't make it to the Baseball Hall of Fame in Cooperstown. Shame on me.

29) I wrote a majority of this book in October 2012 during a four-week hideout at Kyle's family cabin in the Sierra Nevada Mountains. Secluded halfway between Sacramento and Lake Tahoe, it was my loneliest and most productive month of the year.

30) With coincidental timing, I happened to be in San Francisco throughout the entire 2012 World Series. On the day of the Giants' championship parade, I skipped it, and instead drove around other parts of San Francisco defiantly waving my Padres hat out the window. If only I had Harry The Heckler hanging out the passenger side...

Lastly, I would like to extend a heartfelt "THANK YOU" to the many people who made an incredible impact on my journey. My trip wouldn't have been the same, and maybe not possible, without these folks (in chronological order):

- Crazy BMW Girl (Los Angeles, CA)
- Kyle (hosted in Miami, FL – 3x)
- Cranberry, Mikey, Ivan & Hagen (Marlins Park)
- Mom (Temecula, CA)
- Brandon, Julie, Malia & Isla (Chula Vista, CA)
- AJ & Kevin (Angel Stadium of Anaheim)
- Mitch & Sean (Hermosa Beach & Studio City, CA)
- Kyle's brother Ryan (Westwood, CA)
- Dave, Karen, Stevie, Brysant & Tia (Danville, CA)
- Susan (O.co Coliseum)

- Dad (Santa Cruz, CA)
- Mirtha, Corina & Natalia (Pacific Grove, CA)
- Kurt, Robin, Stan, Carolee, Kyle & Phil (Saratoga, CA)
- Elliot, Andy, Russi, Brent, Taba, Tom, Matt, Beef, Summer, Allison, Hannah & Kim (San Francisco, CA)
- The MFCHS Crew (Lake Wildwood, CA)
- Todd & Amy (Bainbridge Island, WA)
- Uncle Brent (Portland, OR)
- Grandpa, Gail, Jay, Roy & Cathy (Salem, OR)
- The Cook Family, Kristen & Amie (Centennial, CO)
- Billy & Joleen (Lenexa, KS)
- Ross & Lindsey (Couchsurfing hosts in Minneapolis, MN)
- Rob, Connie & Damien (Miller Park)
- Mikey, Neil, Ivan, Amy & Morgan (Chicago, IL)
- Katie (The Westin St. Louis)
- Ed (Couchsurfing host in St. Louis, MO)
- Ted, David & Lyuba (Couchsurfing friends in Atlanta, GA)
- Steve (Turner Field & Tropicana Field)
- Kenny (Great American Ballpark)
- Samantha (Couchsurfing host in Cincinnati, OH)
- Tales (Couchsurfing host in Detroit, MI)
- Aunt Wendy & Hannah (Akron, OH)
- Lauren (All-Star Couchsurfing host in Cleveland, OH)
- Mike (Progressive Field)
- The Ludwig Family (PNC Park)
- Bryan (Philadelphia Marriott Downtown)
- Kristen & Bea (Philadelphia, PA)
- Emily, Colin & Family (Landisville, PA)
- Vic & Janet (Milford, CT)

- Sarah (Brooklyn, NY)
- Carrie (New York, NY)
- The Vopelak Family (Clifton Park, NY)
- Kevin, Nicole & her family (Acton, MA)
- Kristen (Boston, MA)
- The Jures Family (from Temecula, CA)
- Ashley & Mike (Washington, D.C.)
- Louis (Hyatt Regency Capitol Hill)
- Mallory, Adam, Corey, Austin & Andy (Miami, FL)
- Lou at Bohemian Café (St. Petersburg, FL)
- Kyle, Anne, Sarah, Lisa (Austin, TX)
- Andrew & Claire (Dallas, TX)
- Uncle Mark, Aunt Debbie, Chelsea & Christine (Houston, TX)
- Grandpa & Grandma (Kerrville, TX)
- Uncle Doug, Darlene & Family (Phoenix, AZ)
- Ben & Alanna (Tampa, FL)
- AJ & Nicole (Temecula, CA)
- Chuck Brodsky (songwriter of *The Ballad Of Eddie Klepp*)

CHAPTER 36
A Final Word

Since finishing my trip, people keep asking me the exact same question: "What was the best ballpark?" No matter where I go – parties, restaurants, barbecues – it always comes up, without fail, like clockwork. It's quite annoying actually, because it's an impossible question to answer. So I tell everyone the same thing: They're all unique. They're all special. They each have their own teams, their own fans, and their own place in history, all of which fuse into a cultural landmark that can't be replicated.

Although hearing this question is repetitive, predictable, and entirely subjective, I enjoy responding to it because it indicates something awesome about our country. It tells me that people care very deeply about this game. They could ask me about the thirty-seven states that I bussed through, the random couches that I slept on, or the shenanigans that I found myself in, but they don't. People ask about the ballparks. Their interest lies in baseball.

Masked on their faces, though, is usually a desperate plea for more. They're thirsty for the story. They dream of what I felt. That's when I tell them about this book, my untold tale of baseball, adventure, and life, tightly seamed together like red threads into white leather.

You're probably thinking, whoa, back up, what about the Kaufman Ballpark Index? Shouldn't that decipher the "best" ballpark in baseball? No. Opinions are opinions, and mine are based off one experience at one game, distributed across nine self-chosen categories. That's not the American democracy we've come to rely on. That's monarchy.

Sure, there's an assumed consensus that some ballparks are "better" than others, but I can't name one fanbase that would trade their home field for another ballpark in baseball. At first, the theory of swapping stadiums may sound grandiose – different features, modern design, better amenities – but on second thought, those cities, those fans, would inherit a building that's not their own. It would be laced with some other team's history, some other team's tradition, and some other team's culture.

I'll use the example of the ballparks in San Francisco and Oakland, which, despite only being several miles apart, rank the highest and lowest in the KBI, respectively. Do you think that Oakland, if San Francisco made the offer, would actually trade O.co Coliseum for AT&T Park? Initially, the proposal might sound like a steal, another one of Billy Beane's too-good-to-be-true "Moneyball" orchestrations. But when you really think about it, it's more like getting robbed. It would strip away the memories and history and culture that A's fans associate with their team. Would they be willing to give up their rowdy outfield bleachers, where diehard fans rambunctiously wave huge flags and don ridiculous costumes? Would they be willing to give up Grant Balfour's Ragefest, where fans go berserk to Metallica's "One" whenever he enters the game to pitch the ninth inning? Would the Oakland fans be able to say goodbye to Krazy George and his wild banjo, or

Susan's favorite popcorn chicken? Would the wave of green and gold be willing to stare at World Series banners in orange and black? What about the retired numbers of Reggie Jackson, Ricky Henderson, "Catfish" Hunter, Rollie Fingers, and Dennis Eckersley? Would the fans be willing to give them all up, to instead look at the retired numbers of their rival across the Bay?

When you consider all that, the magnitude and ramification it would place on the heart of the fanbase, there is no way that Oakland, or any other city for that matter, would trade their stadium for anything else in the world. They might build a new one, but they would never swap the unique personality of their beloved ballpark for another. Each city has too much invested emotionally, too much tradition to lose. I guarantee that if San Francisco hypothetically made that offer, the A's would tell the Giants to shove it. You're offering us your "best" ballpark for our "worst"? We don't care. Shove it. This is why the "best ballpark" question is impossible to answer. It's why I tell everyone that the "best" ballpark... is always your own.

As wonderful as it was to experience the history and traditions in each city, my ballpark tour was as much a spiritual journey as it was a baseball one. Despite my usually mum stance on the topic, I discreetly hinted at this notion during several key points throughout the story.

In Chapter One, my references to demons, Hell-A, and Satan's Playground were no coincidence. When I wrote, "I am escaping from this godforsaken cage," I was quietly alluding to the fact that I was out of sorts spiritually. I had lost sight of my future, had fallen off the path that I was supposed to be on, and was living my life without passion. My cycling trek along the California coast and my backpacking excursion through

South America were significant steps in my personal rehabilitation.

In Seattle, and then again in the Tampa finale, I implicated that the "baseball gods" were watching over me from Elysian Fields. These themed associations were intended for entertainment purposes, but they powerfully suggested my overwhelming sense that God was actually watching over me from above. When I shared some of the stories in this book with a friend after my tour, she kept asking me, "How did all these crazy things keep happening to you? Why were you so lucky?" I couldn't sufficiently answer her, but I certainly feel like there were times when angels flew next to me.

Looking back upon my trip, I've considered the relationship between luck versus coincidence versus divine intervention. Was it "luck" that netted me seven free tickets from strangers after I did the same deed in Seattle? Was it just "coincidence" that my Couchsurfing host in Minneapolis randomly welcomed two other people doing the exact same trip? What about in Philadelphia, where a public act of kindness saved me from missing the train to Citizens Bank Park? Or in New York, where I hit rock bottom on 34th Street before miraculously finding a place to stay? Did I simply "luck" out in Washington DC when a storm halted just long enough to squeeze in nine innings of play? And in Boston, was it just "coincidence" that I bumped into a couple from my hometown in California?

"Luck" is defined as success brought by chance outside of one's own actions, while "coincidence" is defined as a remarkable occurrence of events without an apparent causal connection. There is no doubt that my journey was filled with incredible luck and rare coincidences, but where do I draw the line? When I started adding up all of my luck and coincidences over and over and over again, and considered the frequency and perfection in each series of events, it gave me reason to believe that there is something else, a causal connection outside of our own control, that is greater than ourselves. I have faith this is God.

The final moment of my journey was a feeling I will never forget. When B.J. Upton capped off my summer with that improbable, coincidental, come-from-behind, walk-off home run in the bottom of the ninth inning, I felt like I was watching a scene in the movie *Angels In The Outfield*. It was as if golden-winged halos swung the bat and escorted the ball over the fence, looking back at me with a playful expression that poked, "Can you see us now?"

I can only compare the feeling in that moment, the tingles down my spine, to the Buddhist term *nirvana*, the liberation of the soul in an idyllic place. It was like God was my third base coach, waving me around as I circled the bases and headed for home. The déjà-vu ending that night made a believer out of me, that the unlikely sequence of events that brought me back to Tampa wasn't just luck or coincidence. It humbly reminded me that throughout my entire trip, I was simply a rubber ducky being pushed along in a divine bathtub.

I know it's a bit jarring to bring this up at the end of a baseball-themed book, but this was a journey that changed my life. Before I roared out my car like a born-again tiger on that hot afternoon in Los Angeles, I had lost touch with my purpose. I had forgotten what makes me happy. But for whatever reason, when I submerged myself into baseball for an entire summer, and set my sights on writing this book, it provided a new sense of ownership. It fermented me with joy. I put all of my baseballs into one basket, and the game of baseball reciprocated with a gift of its own.

There's also something very humanitarian, even utopian, about going to a baseball game. There isn't one other place in this country, maybe in the world, which attracts so many different people, from so many different backgrounds, all for one cause. As I sat in my seat in Cincinnati, halfway through my trip, it donned on me that the sport of baseball brings together every demographic imaginable: men and women, young and old, rich and poor, white and black, Democrat and Republican, religious and atheist, heterosexual and LGBT. They all sit in peace amongst each other for the sake of baseball, buying Cracker Jacks and hot dogs together at ballparks across America. If that realization doesn't scream red, white, and blue, with thirteen stripes and fifty stars, then I don't know what will. That's the culture of baseball in a peanut shell. That's the beautiful reason it's America's game.

I tried to come up with another place that replicates the American melting pot as much as a baseball congregation. Football stadiums? Too fratty. The DMV? Not everyone drives. Wal-Mart? Filled with Martians. The only other place that I could think of, the only place that's even considerable, is a church, where all kinds of different people, from all kinds of different backgrounds, might gather together for one reason or another. You see, there's a connection. Ballparks aren't merely a place to watch baseball. They're a place where ordinary citizens repair their souls with the blessing of a game. I believe in that now more than ever. I believe that ballparks are houses of God just like churches.

I once heard the Dalai Lama say, "The purpose of our lives is to be happy," and I think the Heavenly Father would be the first person to second that motion. I'd be the third. If God was one of us, as suggested in a song by Joan Osbourne, I believe He would be the most passionate baseball fan alive. As

I mentioned in the Denver chapter, baseball fans love beer, so it makes even more sense why Benjamin Franklin once said, "Beer is living proof that God loves us and wants us to be happy." It's synonymous with, "*Baseball* is living proof that God loves us and wants us to be happy." He used my love for the game to influence and change the direction of my life for the better.

Although this book has been themed around ballparks and baseball, I hope that my personal journey inspires you to never be afraid of change, to never settle for less, to always follow your heart, to chase your dreams, and to pursue happiness as your primary goal in life. While everyone's story is different and unique, I was reminded throughout mine of why we are here and what life is about. It's been an incredible soul-searching ride since Chapter One, and I hope that in sharing my stories with all of you, I've provided as many smiles as I had along the way. My summer journey to all thirty ballparks was my own personal miracle, and I now know that where miracles happen, paradise is found.

About The Author

Cody Kaufman has been entrenched in the sport of baseball since 1989, when he first chucked his baby bottle over the railing at San Diego's Jack Murphy Stadium. He graduated from U.C. Santa Barbara in June 2009, and later moved to Los Angeles after teaching English in Thailand. While driving home from work one afternoon in "Hell-A", Cody underwent a quarter-life crisis that motivated him to leave behind his old life in search of something new. After cycling the California coast and backpacking for three months in South America, Cody returned to the United States to hunt down one of his longtime dreams. During the summer of 2012, he attended a baseball game at all thirty Major League ballparks, a journey that changed his life.

Homegrown in Temecula, California, Cody Kaufman enjoys playing sports, guitar, and cribbage. His favorite teams are the San Diego Padres, San Diego Chargers, Houston Rockets, and Texas Longhorns. He also has future ambitions to attend a football game at every NFL stadium in one season. Cody loves meeting new people, and would be delighted to discuss sports, travel, and writing opportunities with his fans. He may be reached through www.30TicketsToParadise.com.

Made in the USA
San Bernardino, CA
08 December 2015